RANCH STORIES FROM JACKASS ROAD

A COMING-OF-AGE STORY

LISA NORTH

Ranch Stories from Jackass Road: A Coming-of-Age Story

Copyright © 2019 by Lisa North
All rights reserved.

ISBN-13: 978-1-7334496-1-8

No part of this book may be reproduced in any form or by any means electronically or otherwise, unless permission has been granted by the author and/or publisher, with the exception of brief excerpts for review purposes.

Cover creation courtesy of Ravi Verma from https://rdezines.com

Editing and formatting by Lorraine Reguly from www.WordingWell.com

Dedication

This book is dedicated to my family.

"If you don't die of thirst, there are blessings in the desert. You can be pulled into limitlessness, which we all yearn for, or you can do the beauty of minutiae, the scrimshaw of the tiny and precise. The sky is your ocean, and the crystal silence will uplift you like great gospel music, or Neil Young."

~Anne Lamott

RANCH STORIES FROM JACKASS ROAD

Table of Contents

Author's Note.. 7

Prologue 9

Chapter 1: The First Night 13

Chapter 2: Shock and Awe 19

Chapter 3: Addresses, Indians, and Motorcycles... 25

Chapter 4: Mrs. Johnston and Dittos vs. Cords...... 31

Chapter 5: "I'll Have You Know, I Walked for Miles in the Snow, When I Was Your Age!".................... 41

Chapter 6: Swings and Soul Things........................ 47

Chapter 7: Rodents Are Not Nice Bedfellows........ 51

Chapter 8: Pacific Palisades Debutante 55

Chapter 9: Go-Carts, Coyotes, and Brothers.......... 67

Chapter 10: White Bull Named Dennis 73

Chapter 11: Hippie Cousins, Barn Life, and Porch Shrines 79

Chapter 12: Neighbors and Distant Relatives 87

Chapter 13: Indian Relics and Haunted Shacks..... 91

Chapter 14: Goats, Gottingers, and Butchered Pigs 97

Chapter 15: Pets, Sort Of 103

Chapter 16: Illegal in the Barn 109

Chapter 17: Robby, Rosie, and the Third Wheel .. 115

Chapter 18: Where's my Red Cape? 121

Chapter 19: Renovation 101 127

Chapter 20: Something Strange in the Night Sky . 133

Chapter 21: Barn Birth 139

Chapter 22: The Boy Who Lived in a Shoe 145

Chapter 23: The Cousin 155

Chapter 24: Planes, Trains, and Autopilot 163

Chapter 25: All Good Things Come to an End, I Guess… 167

Epilogue 171

About the Author 173

Author's Note

All of the characters and stories in this book are based on real events and people. However, names have been changed to protect the autonomy of those involved, and some events and details have been altered slightly for the integrity of the (mostly) linear storyline.

LISA NORTH

Prologue

We buried my dad on Jackass Road.

No one would have laughed louder at the irony of this than he would have. I could actually hear his chuckles wafting up from the scabby, dry pebbles where we deposited him in all his ashen glory. We didn't exactly bury him. Instead, we poured him out, as an offering to the desert sanctum that had claimed all of our lives.

*****

I had gotten the call at three in the morning—the one that pulls you out of a dream and leaves you searching for an alarm that didn't go off—from my sister, who is not usually in the habit of calling at that time. When I woke, I saw there were two missed calls. A dread of cold flooded my senses and I braced myself.

I had received a similar phone call just three years prior, from my brother, who was calling from a scratchy mountain phone connection that crumbled his words in between his tears. He called once to say my mom was at the hospital and to pray. Then, just a half hour later, he called again, to say she was gone. Not gone, like on a trip, but gone, for good. That's what death feels like. The person just disappears and isn't here anymore, like an expat to another universe you can't reach.

I thought I'd never recover from that call—that interruption of everything I thought I understood—so I knew what to expect this time… except, not really.

With a sort of reluctant confidence, I called my sister back.

"Dad was rushed to the hospital…," she began. The details fell into broken pieces and pounded in my ears. Her words came in between birdlike gasps. "He's gone."

Not again!

No, he's not. He can't just call down his exit like that—in a "drop the mic, and I'm out" fashion!

Is this some grand, last word, Dad? Are you directing this finale for your own glory? Maybe it's just an all-out mutiny because life didn't look quite how it was supposed to.

All the "just yesterdays" came tripping in, looking for a railing to grip. I dismissed them. He couldn't just leave… not when we were finally getting to the good stuff—you know, when you finally begin to see your parents as human and begin to develop compassion instead of angst—who take on shape with mistakes that look almost comical instead of derogatory. We had actually just begun to see a few things under the same kind of light. His refracted a little more than mine, but I was getting there.

I faded in and out of my sister's tin voice on the other end of the line as I began to remember when he and I had coffee and talked about photons of light that leave your body when you die. He was really into stuff like that—I call it esoteric metaphysical physics. He was always talking about what was next, on the other side, where God and all the answers live. String theory with knots that keep us tethered here, while all the "untethered souls" fly home to the bosom of the Great Spirit in the sky. He was perpetually sitting on the edge of this life, looking off and out to an unknown something over there, calling out to it with longing, like a gull seeking a better shore.

As my sister's voice died out, I began to remember everything and nothing but quite a literal spot, at the end of a dilapidated porch, on the edge of nowhere—my dad's favorite place in the world.

*****

Now, here we were, back at that place, coming full circle. Classic Dad.

*****

There was a time, years ago, when he had decided he was done with life… or, at least, with the status quo. He had heard the call of the wild. It was guttural, more like a yank, and he had to follow it. How he shaped our lives from that call, he literally will never know.

As I stood at the base of ash, I looked out to the "Ranch" he loved so much. I want to untether myself and join him, for just a bit, to see what he sees now, to know what he now knows, to see the face of God, and see if He looks like how I can never picture, but always see. I want to be there with him, but all I seem to be able to do instead of cry is remember. I see those few tenuous years on this barren patch play out before me—*Yes, Dad, like a great Shakespearean play*. I guess we are all just mere players, after all.

*****

There is a breezy delirium to the wild sagebrush that blisters the hillsides of the high desert, like the first sip of coffee or a slap on the face. Maybe it stampedes the imagination; trips it up, like a child spins around, just to feel dizzy. I drank in this stark freshness in gulps and found my center in its harsh sweetness. The stories to follow are footnotes to those impressions and a tribute to the man that decided to take us there. If there's one predictable element about life in the desert, it's that it is unpredictable and you either collide with it, or ebb in its flow. I think, as a girl of twelve, I did both.

Chapter 1: The First Night

Mom was getting married—again.

In our broken home scenario, this simply meant the pegs had just shifted and we got bumped. The new husband had to take precedence. I got it.

Mom had a new gleam in her eye; a spring in her giddy step. She deserved it, but we just couldn't bear to play second fiddle, not again. To my sister, brother, and me, this merely begged the question, "So what does Dad have to offer, this go-around?"

We had just spent the weekend with him doing "Divorce-Dad, fun stuff." I think it was the fair; at least, I always associate the fair with "Dad weekends." He was candy-apples and scary rides I forced myself to go on. Two days never went faster.

Then it was back home, to Mom, the treacherous war zone we like to call school, and babysitters that cooked tortillas with weird things in them.

Dad always had a "new ballgame," his coined phrase for a new and usually tempting plan. He was the bad-ass coach of all time! And now that Mom was heading into her newly found wedded bliss, he laid out for us his newest and grandest yet.

He had just purchased a forty-acre ranch in the high desert of California and was retiring from his law practice for a while, to "find himself," I supposed. It wasn't until much later that he shared the catalyst for this decision. One of the clients he had defended had revealed insider information. Basically, the guy narced on his former gang members and the crimes they were involved in, some of whom resided in the penitentiary the judge decided to send him to for a couple of months, "to teach him a lesson." My dad pleaded with the judge, knowing that his client would not survive the two months. He didn't.

So, Dad bought two green motorcycles, a ranch, and a little time off.

In my mind's eye, which, by the way, is usually not the most reliable source, he was to build a "Bonanza Ponderosa," sort of a "Little House on the Prairie." At least that's how I viewed it with my limited, television-addicted schema, and he wanted us to "Come with!" In light of our current deportation from top of the Mom rung, this proposition sounded pretty good; fair-days with Dad all of the time!

We packed our bags, which was pretty much like rote for us, and said our goodbyes to Mom. Her wedded bliss just got the wind knocked out of it. She had tears and I had second thoughts. She was my whole world, really, but then I had a realization. *Now she would be "Weekend Mom" and would get a shot at being the novelty!*

As she gathered her Kleenex into her sleeve, her warm coffee cup hands gripped mine.

"Make sure to do your homework and, you know, take care of your little brother. He can get a little lost." I knew what she meant.

Her red, puffy eyes reminded me of all the times we would say goodbye to Grandma as she'd stand on the road edge until we drifted away.

"You'll come for weekends, Mom, and we'll dance and listen to The Supremes and everything we always do," is what I wanted to say, but all the faculties I possessed, just to keep my own tears sucked in, were being used up. So, I just held on and nodded.

I climbed into our covered wagon-truck, gripped my window-frame Mom, who looked a little lost herself, and held my brother's dimpled hand tight. It's done now, I thought, no turning back.

It was like when I was five and threatened to run away…

I had packed my bag with the essentials: a blanket, the silken slip I would rub between my fingers against my cheek, and a Twinkie. I was ready to brave the world outside my mama's kitchen.

She came into my room as I was packing.

"So, you look pretty ready to go. Do you need some help packing?"

Disarmed, I replied, "I'm fine. I'm going to Grandma's." I was brave and defiant.

"Ok, so that's about 20 miles from here, so make sure you wear good walking shoes. Do you want me to make you a sandwich?"

I was pretty hungry; I could feel the growl in my stomach.

"Ok. Thanks."

"Sure, honey. I love you and I don't want you to starve to death on your long trek to Grandma's."

I was packed and ready. I would walk out the big door, into the big world, leaving my mama in the doorway. As I turned the corner, I started thinking about how she smelled of cigarettes, Doublemint gum, and hairspray all mushed together in a really great way. I thought how I could cuddle up to that smell tonight while watching Brady Bunch and eating popcorn from a bowl.

Then, you guessed it, I came racing back to find her, arms open and ready for me to change my mind.

This time, though, we turned the corner and I wondered if she was still standing in the doorway with her arms open, waiting for me to turn the corner with my slip between my fingers. But I chose Dad, and now I was stuck. So, I rolled the window down for a new smell of a new country, where Dad was king—Fair Days Dad.

What I didn't realize was that fair days with Dad were going to be more like the scary rides I didn't want to go on than the candy apples. It began to feel like all the camping trips we would take over the years with Grandma and Grandad. I would stand on the edge of the shoreline of whatever lake we camped beside, biting my fingernails, desperately not wanting to give in to any of my uncle's coercion, to finally try some adventure, usually some new type of diving for the first time. Those nervous pangs would become my constant companions for the next several years, but I would dive in anyway. The water would shock me, but I would get used to it and jump again and again.

At age twelve, I wish I could say that I was a second-glance, pre-teen beauty. Reality bites, and the awkward funk that was me is rather painful to describe, but here goes. I was straight up and down; a wide, plank-like squishy flooring. Hips were lost in what my mom still called baby fat. I had a couple of bumps out front, but they looked misplaced without the hips, like nodules or tumors. They just stood there, ashamed at being left on such a construct. I was dishwater blonde (every time I did the dishes I'd think, that's what my hair looks like!) with a perpetual frizz ball in the back that would not yield to any powers or products. Then there were the freckles; countless connect-the-dots. I thought if I could just clump them together, I might actually look tan for once—or, even better, Native, which would have come in handy as I went to school with all the Indian kids from the reservation. (I could call them Native Americans, but they would have kicked my ass for that.) I was an underdeveloped, freckled, frizz ball only a mother could love. Hopefully, Weekend Dad would, too.

I see her now—that awkward, insecure girl of twelve—and want to tell her that she will have real moments of glory, where all the stars and hips align. Time will stand at attention while she stumbles, climbs, dreams, and clamors after life, God, and love, in all of its pain and loveliness.

For now, she is about to go on one wild ride.

Chapter 2: Shock and Awe

My older sister, my little bro (who was already decked out in his Ponderosa uniform), and I were crammed into a two-seater truck. Cars began to sift away as we edged closer to our destination. This life-altering experience for my brother would never take leave of him, like a Veteran and his war. Even far into his adult years, he would go out to the ranch to be, to think, to forget, and to try to reclaim himself.

I thrust my face to the window wind, letting the night filter in, letting go of certainty's grip to the looser chains of uncertainty's drunken bite.

As we approached the road that led to our new home, the landscape opened up wider than my imagination. The hills looked like a child drew them, like in *Harold with His Crayon*; perfectly rounded, with clumps of boulders and craggy lone oaks guarding the tempered grasses. They began to become silhouettes of themselves by nightfall, so my mind filled them in. The air began to balloon up with the punch of sage wind, and I knew I was somewhere that chases and always catches you.

We turned onto our dirt road. It was blacker than when you close yourself up in a closet to hide from everything. Nighttime is darker and more visceral in the desert; it is a night you feel, and stars are not mere trinkets like Christmas lights but rather like blasts of lightning, making everyone astronomers.

Our road was dusty and weathered by the countless spring flash floods that were so deeply creviced by them that you felt as if you could fall in. Ahead of us was nothing but our headlights, cupped by the night.

All of a sudden, blazing in front of us in zany zigzags, were rabbits! Not bunnies, but long-eared things; jackrabbits they're called, kin to desert nights. They long-bounded into our headlights like double-dutch jump ropers—nocturnal acrobats announcing our entrance.

We approached our "ranch house." It was a one-room, adobe brick building. I looked around for the rest of it, but that was it. The blessing of limited light allowed my sensibilities to remain hopeful. Unfortunately, the weather didn't help much. Like a hibernating bear awoken, weather in the desert can change on a dime. Because it was February, a blast of snow began to bellow at us. The desert is such a drama queen—nothing is ever calm; everything is in extremes. I would later discover how this actually paralleled my father's own internal topography. These two were kindred spirits to one another. I don't think he realized that at the time, but I began to see the similarities immediately. Uncertainty and spontaneity are great rollercoaster buddies, but not exactly the best security blankets. The temperament of the man that was blazing our trail was full of surprises, for sure, indelible in their stain and yet philosophically burrowed into us like a Sahara sunset.

The snow began to wail. A blizzard was beginning to incubate the land. The result would be eight-foot snowdrifts in the morning. As we walked in, I surveyed the gray, dank walls and matching cement floors. I bit my lip to hold in the tears. I wanted to turn the corner as all of my delusions of grandeur slipped away like desert rabbits. I briefly wondered what Mom and Husband #3 were doing but I quickly dismissed that thought and braced myself for a lonely night.

I woke up the next morning, cocooned in fungi-woven wool blankets, five of them (I counted). They were my protectors from the arctic blast that had whistled its way through the gray adobe walls. Adobe? What is it? It resembled cellblocks in prison movies I'd seen. This little one-room house was akin to a four-walled penitentiary cell. I was beginning to hope the resemblance stopped there. The floors were ice cold. I'm not sure about the ceiling. It was solid and devoid of holes. (It would be for a while, until we decided to renovate, then it would have plastic canopies filled with rain pockets. Our morning ritual would then involve emptying them.)

The hearth was a behemoth of a thing. It was our life source; almost like an oracular Lamaze tool, teaching us to breathe, just breathe.

"So, what do ya think? Cool, huh?" Dad prodded as I tried to wipe the sleep frozen on my eyelids.

"Yup, cool Dad. Cold, actually." I attempted my best lighthearted jest so as to not reveal the sinking pit in my stomach, soon to surface in my eyes if I didn't avert it.

He walked away just in time and didn't see it all begin to well up.

Tears were strictly forbidden, at least in my personal code of conduct, with Dad. He was British, through and through. He practically plastered the flag to his chest. He would belt out short excerpts from *God Save the Queen.* He never quite knew all the words to any song he attempted, so baritone mumbled hums would quickly follow any minstrel attempts. Then he would switch to *The Silver-Tongued Devil and I,* in his low, Kris Kristofferson-like warbles. You get the picture. Needless to say, his English boarding school upbringing would not tolerate yellow streaks or spineless lip quivers. Keeping a stiff upper lip was the *modus operandi*. Later, however, as he became age-ripened, life's memories would find their way into his eyes, and the floods would come. I would watch in awe and think, *No fair!*

"Fire's on its way. Did you sleep okay?" Dad was not a stupid man; he could see the panic in my face as well as the ice crystals forming on the corners of my mouth. "Hey, how's about a bit of bacon and *tomauto,* and a cup a tea? Nothin' like a good cup a tea to fix all that ails."

I nodded and looked around for my brother and sister. They were up and exploring. I began to wonder if they were feeling the weight of what we'd gotten ourselves into as well. Do they still see Mom in the doorway with her Kleenex-filled, bulging sleeve?

I wasn't really feeling the call of the wild just yet. I wanted to stay buried in my prison blankets instead and wait for Britain to descend in the form of Dad's breakfast.

Since youth's disillusionments are brief, and adventure is the sweet tooth of childhood, I began to realize that the *Ponderosa* was back *on the Prairie* with *The Little House,* attended to by all the anecdotes of Hoss and Little Joe. I was obviously, as previously discussed, not a *half-pint,* either. All of the raucous moments to come—from rusty on/off water to rattlesnakes in the bathtub, armies of mice warring for land rights, and even "BM's" (AKA "number twos") in the snow—would give us an awareness; a heightened sense of the world that we could claim as our own… and did, and still do.

LISA NORTH

Chapter 3: Addresses, Indians, and Motorcycles

There was a brief adjustment before the inevitable killjoy—school—was about to normalize our adventure, or so I thought. What I didn't realize was that school, too, would be filled with color and tinged with edge. In all of the giddiness of the "new ballgame," it had completely slipped my mind that I was to start a new school… again.

*****

One day, recently, over coffee, my sister and I counted how many schools we each had attended while growing up. We decided we could send army brats shamefully into hiding with their tails between their legs. Thirty was my count. Hers was a little less, primarily because she did less bouncing between parents than I did. My folks were all about change—change of landscape, change of address, and often even change of faces. Together, counting marriages and live-ins, it requires two hands to count. Home, for me, was Grandma's house. It was the one stationary element in the collage of change. Don't get me wrong, life was never dull, and I learned some skills!

*****

Let's just say I had become a professional new-school goer. But this new homegrown K-8 desert school (there weren't enough kids for a separate middle school) would bring its own challenges to my professionalism. For one thing, transportation had its own obstacles to unleash. Our adobe abode was a good mile and a half from the main road, hence the green motorcycles that came with us on the move.

My sister became quite the biker chick at thirteen. She would drive a motorcycle and I would ride on the seat behind her, clasping her for dear life, oftentimes with blinding stinging slow flakes blasting our faces or mosquitos we'd have to pick out of our teeth before boarding the bus. As our icy or bug-laden freedom flew by us, at thirty-five miles an hour, I felt the glory of the nighttime rabbits. That short mile-and-a-half was a tesseract to another universe, where my sister was the hero, catalyst, and conduit for our wild adventure. She would navigate the crevices in the road with a boisterous and contagious laugh; her vernacular like an innate creature that knows its habitat.

My sister is an extraordinary woman.

She has curly, dark hair and curls in her personality. She is all optimism and positivity. I don't think I've ever seen her distraught, except when Dad passed. He was her compass.

Needless to say, I had total confidence in this iconic wonder. She was fail-proof. She could master anything and I hung on her coattails, literally. In fact, I found my balance there. She was my certainty.

Whenever I was solo, she was my imaginary friend. Five foot-one in four-inch heels, she stands tall, and big-busted, like a little Eastern European powerhouse that could slap you with a sausage and seduce with flirty charm, she was, and is, a ball-buster with angel eyes. So, it was natural that I would put my life into her hands, every day, on our bus stop race-for-your-life course. We only had one dump in all those comings and goings, and I have to say I cherish the scar on my leg that came from the exhaust pipe that seared my flesh that indelible day, which left water blisters the size of large grapes. That mark is a sweet memento I can reach down and touch on a mundane day filled with normal.

We would arrive at the bus stop, at the end of our dirt road, and hide the green motorcycle behind a green eucalyptus tree. Like a faithful dog, it would be waiting there for us when we returned.

The bus ride to our new school was forty-five minutes long. Our fellow commuters became our intimate comrades as we shared our lives together. One particular guy on that bus was a full-blooded Indian (as he would tell us, way too often) named Johnny Ramirez, who had thick, ink-black hair and football shoulders.

I fell in and out of love with Johnny because he was all sweetness and toughness and had the whitest smile that filled his eyes up.

We would all listen to Johnny as he told us stories about his uncles and cousins on the "Rez," who got drunk every night and then proceeded to get into fights all the time.

"Not me, man. That's not gonna be me," he would say.

Then, one day, Johnny showed up with a black eye. He didn't have stories that day or a white smile.

After a while, Johnny stopped commuting with us. He would show up now and then, and fade into the back of the bus, eyes slanted in rhythmic droops with the bumps and swerves of the bus. I wonder, to this day, where my white smiling full-blooded Indian friend is and if he is someone's uncle or cousin.

Addresses scribble down our permanence and claim our landlocked days and nights. I think all of us long for boat whistles and runways and commutes to the unusual and unpredictable.

Johnny just wanted off the reservation, as did most of the kids I went to school with. Their goals were not so much a "running to," but more like a running away from; a green motorcycle to somewhere else. For me, I was there already; a place to run both away from and to… a crazy address with a P.O. box and a dirt road with a green motorcycle.

LISA NORTH

Chapter 4: Mrs. Johnston and Dittos vs. Cords

I sifted [handwritten note covering text: "idolizes her sister, wants to be like her, in a different class"]
came ea
or, in m

Part of t
my teacher. She was the coolest. My sister and I ended up in the same class together, even though she was in eighth grade and I was in sixth. It was the "honors" class but I just thought it was a testament to my maturity and wisdom beyond my natural years that I was in a class with eighth-graders. Mrs. Johnston was blonde, tan, smart and going through a divorce. We benefited from her crisis because she thrust herself into us, her progeny.

Every day had an out of the ordinary twist to it. Learning, to her, was a "life thing" more than a "book thing," which made her especially grand to a sixth-grader that was not exactly into the book thing either. We talked about meaning and discussed poetry and current issues and whatever the hell was going on in *Lord of the Flies.* We went on weird field trips to odd places. One, in particular, stands out. It was a trip to a mausoleum and cemetery. We actually did a tour of the crematorium. (This tour came to mind, surfacing from my collective subconscious, no doubt, as a frame of reference regarding my parents, when we cremated them. I thought, *Oh, I know how they do that!*)

Divorce must feel just a tad bit like death, and that tour might have been Mrs. Johnston's "Sylvia Plath moment." Perhaps it was the actual week she signed the papers. Like good progenies, we hid our apprehension of the morbid and talked about how interesting and awe-inspiring it was to hear the crematorium guy tell us about the 80-something-year-old woman he'd just finished up before we came. None of us talked or ate for the rest of the day.

Crematorium field trips aside, we thought Mrs. Johnston was simply the best.

This was no ordinary class! Not only did we travel to eccentric places, but we also got to enlist in "Mrs. Johnston's Cooking Class." We made black flapjacks—buckwheat, I believe—and biscuits that were life-altering little fluffs of carb-y goodness.

Then there was the cactus apple jelly. I collected the apples. Of course, these "orchard fruits" required gloves and gas burners to singe the spikes off before scooping the pulp into batches of what would become the most scrumptious flavored jelly one ever tasted. My brother still talks about the cactus apple jelly, resembling a cross-between fresh baby strawberries with the dark, rich, tarty tang of rhubarb mushed in. Naturally, the jelly went well with the biscuits we had for lunch. Silently eating on the lawn of the cemetery, life never tasted so good.

Mrs. Johnston was an original, and I so wanted to be her. I think I'd even have taken on her divorce. Somehow, it made her seem even more cosmopolitan. Having my own expertise in such matters, I could have added some panache to the travail. My sis and I actually had a plan to keep Mrs. Johnston in our lives: we would set her up with Dad.

He saw her one day when he picked us up from school and decided she was "not half bad," so he said, "Sure, why not? What the hell, I'll take her out. What's the worst that could happen?" he chuckled, knowing full well the worst thing that could happen—she'd fall for him and then get dumped before she even had a moment to know what hit her.

My dad loved women and respected them with egalitarian equanimity, at least, in the broad scheme of things.

He appreciated strong independence and acute-mindedness, as long as the package was in great form. He never fell for a Bambi or a Tiffany.

They were all thoughtful, lovely, intelligent women to emulate, particularly my mom, who never really got over him completely but remained his one true friend to the end.

That being said, Dad was pretty cavalier about his women. They would traipse in and, after his charm and wit wore through, they would traipse back out, or he would, in an absolute matter-of-fact manner, boot them out. He would quickly tire of them, yet, somehow, he was able to make them think it was their idea that they'd be better off without him. Much to my own surprise, they usually were. Sometimes, they would resurface. Perhaps they would experience momentary Alzheimer's and just his wit would come to mind, so they'd come back for more.

We could never figure out how he got these young, beautiful women to fall for him. He was bald and nowhere near the height he held himself to be. It must have been his Sean Connery likeness. In fact, after the gray settled into his beard, people would come up to him and relay the remarkable resemblance, then he would roll out his "Grrrawmpa Deave" with his baritone Scottish brogue firmly in place, much to the delight of his grandkids.

Dad had a way with the female population and we wanted him to work his charms on our future stepmom, Mrs. Johnston.

Of course, we just knew Mrs. Johnston would be different; she was the one! We had our whole lives mapped out: the dresses we'd wear at the wedding, the Funkadelic trips we'd take as a family (now in the clutches of bliss, there would no longer be Sylvia Plath types, we hoped), and we just knew she'd work perfectly on the ranch (unlike his next wife, who was ten years his junior and from Malibu, excuse me, Pacific Palisades; Malibu's older, more sophisticated debutante sister—but that's another chapter). Their date however, was a bit of a dud—at least, on his part. We had waited with bated breath, and that was all we got.

At school, she would ask us about him with a sort of desperation you don't usually get to see in teachers' faces. It was harder to look at her after that. It was especially painful for me because I had found a bit of myself in her face. That was lost now, due to Dad's indifference toward her and consequently her latent indifference to us. I was beginning to keep a tally of "Things lost, due to Dad's lack of, well, Dadness."

****

School life was also full of the typical things that scar our psyches and make us painfully insecure, always itching for acceptance.

The Indians we went to school with lived on the Rez and would clump together on the playground. The eighth-grade boys had mustaches and smoked cigarettes (several had been eighth-graders for a couple of years) and the girls wore cords—corduroys—in muted colors, with muted T-shirts. Most of us outsiders were mute around them.

One girl, in particular—May was her name (sounds bright and springy, huh?!)—had a vendetta against all un-corduroyed patrons that dared to walk the grounds. I wore mine faithfully, every day, and avoided all disdain, carefully mapping out my route to the swings.

One day, there was a new girl, who came from the far-off land of San Diego. She wore bright colors and a life-altering pair of pants called Dittos. Ditto jeans came in a variety of colors and sported a signature U-turn saddle stitch down the backside. They were all the rage down in Diego. Not here, though, and May would crush her, soon enough. I tried to warn her and all the vibrancy of her color, but then something happened. More Dittos showed up on the backsides of even a couple of the Indian girls!

I was ashamed at my conformity when I decided I would try to talk my mom into buying a pair for me. Mom was now Weekend Mom and also our connection to the outside world.

Fashion trends are sort of like green things that get stuck in your teeth that no one tells you are there, such as the pants that hang below junior high school boys' butts, for example. I theorized that mechanics must have come up with this trend and that their sons who happened to ride skateboards decided the coolness factor for them. Or, how about super skinny jeans when you're not exactly, well, you know, super skinny? Dittos were the "it" factor for a season or two, at least, for tweens, in the late '70s, after bell bottoms had lost their panache.

Dittos were highlighters. They magnified the beautiful as well as the ugly. They went all the way to your belly button and, for the most part, were plain and simple cotton pants except for the adorable stitching on the bootie, which was like a little road map on your tushie. For the taut, developed blondes that had tushies like baby cheeks, they were a little frame that said, "Hi there!" However, for those of us with, say, a little more miles to cover on their road maps, they said, "Please just keep walking and excuse me while I sit for a moment!" Nevertheless, I got a pair.

I was so excited!

When I examined my roadmap at home, my exuberance at finally having my very own Dittos convinced me that the image reflecting back at me in the mirror, with the aid of a little squint here and there, looked pretty travel-friendly. I bounced off the bus, ecstatic, in my favorite squirrel T-shirt (yes, I said "squirrel T-shirt," because squirrels are cool, OK?!) and pale pink Dittos! Then "Rosie the Radiant," the pride of the Rez, showed up in the same pair on the same day, and the time space continuum altered, at least, for this traveler.

Not even May could contend against Rosie's glory. She walked in slow motion, I swear, with perfect, lilting, obsidian curls and pale pink Dittos with a roadmap to Little Big Horn!

Suddenly, I was in a desolate, barren no-man's land, where maps cease to have meaning. It was then that I realized that maybe May was onto something, so we hung out on the swings at recess together for the next week, me in my over-washed gray cords and her in her dirt-brown prototypes, dissing the stupid new girl's pants and her complacent posse.

We didn't mention Rosie. She was excluded, obviously. Damn it.

Something happened that week.

I had crossed over. I was no longer the new girl. I was May's bud, conformity licking its lips, a bad-ass chick from the Rez, hanging with the "in" crowd—or, at least, the "in" person; my own personal bodyguard against isolation.

My pretty pink Dittos were stashed away, well-hidden in the bottom of my closet, along with some of the roadmap to myself.

Along the way, though, something happened that caused me to reconsider my shameful, conformist, corduroy-laden self. I made a best friend named Caroline.

Caroline lived at the end of the road near our motorcycle-parking bush, in a simple, little white house. Caroline was a simple, little white girl who wore barrettes, lace-trimmed sweaters, and well-aligned socks. I mention her socks because mine were stained and never even. Also, I was serendipitously fortunate if they ever matched at all.

To look at her, Caroline appeared as though she were from another era, a more proper, clandestine time with things in order and lovelies all around. But all rose-colored eras have their nemesis, and so did Caroline.

She was dry, like her desert life. By dry, I don't mean her wit, but her skin. She had a disease or allergy or something that made her skin resemble the harsh land we occupied. I would look at the intricate lace trim of her sweater just above her crackly, scuffed-up, flaky arm and I'd wonder if her scaly skin would catch on the lace and hurt, then I'd wonder how many pieces of Scotch tape it could fill up with skin cells (it was a long bus ride).

Mostly, I would wonder how she weathered all the ridicule, judgments, and disdain. She was just very matter-of-fact about it.

Maybe, when adversity is a constant companion, it becomes almost like a fair-weather friend—someone you wouldn't necessarily miss if they were gone—yet who never leaves and becomes a fixture, like furniture, and so you adjust. But it was Caroline's joy that was contagious and drew you to her. I loved being around her, in spite of the snickering and spit wads that came from the back of the bus. When the school day was over,

Caroline and I would walk—freckle-armed and scabby-armed—together, belting out, at the tops of our lungs, "*B-b-b-b-Bennie and the Jets*," setting the pace for our own era, one of nonconformity, lace sweaters, and unmatched socks.

Chapter 5: "I'll Have You Know, I Walked for Miles in the Snow, When I Was Your Age!"

Winter rolled through and the motorcycle was retired for a while due to the massive snowdrifts that curved the road into marshmallow mounds high above the beltline. Getting from here to there became a difficult daily routine. Weather in the desert is like an angry husband in your face; you can't move to one side or the other without a little fury spit in your eye. Winter was abusive and dramatic, yet lovely. The exception was when you had to walk home in canvas K-Mart tennis shoes with a little three-year-old cowboy in tow, who you have to carry because his boots don't have socks.

Dad was supposed to pick us up from the local store, which was simply the "everything you need so you don't die" store with access to life on other planets. It consisted of a gas station, post office, and limited grocery items, but it was an exciting outing for us! We had an imperative candy/cacao run to make if we were to hunker down with the hearth and nothing else but the hibernating rodents as company.

Dad, however, forgot about us, so we had a choice to make: hang out at the now boring hole-in-the-wall grocery store or try to make our way up the snow-doused road, back to the house.

We were desperate for our hearth and cacao, and though Mr. Crosby, who ran the General Store, had a few good stories, we'd heard them already and his Waylon Jennings impression was getting a little tiresome by now because, well, it was just too damn cold for impersonations of crusty old cowboy singers.

I already had a two-foot, hungry, tired and cold cowboy at my feet to contend with, so we decided to start on our way.

Exuberance at the adventure carried us for a while. We began to scale the traverse ahead. We had walked the one-and-a-half-mile trek from the General Store back to our house many times, but never like this. The terrain was all a pillow-top of white because the road had disappeared and had blended in with the fields. Only the tops of the snow-crusted cacti that dotted the line cut off for the road kept us on track.

I'd toss my little brother into the snow and he'd giggle. But optimism began to wane at about the half-mile point after my toes had become numb stubs and the cowboy on my back began to be a wailing, cumbersome clump of baggage. You see, my brother saw the ranch as his epoch, his grand and great Cowboy and Indian movie where he was the star. He never went anywhere without his cowboy boots. Oftentimes, all he would have on were his boots and, of course, the accompanying Stetson that dwarfed him in his imagination.

This particular scene, though, was a bit more than he bargained for.

We had to stop for a minute every few steps and eat one or two Sugar Babies, rationing them so we wouldn't have to eat each other.

"Lisa, are we gonna make it?" Derrick attempted, between gasps.

"I'm not sure. You know, if the coyotes hear you blubbering, they're going to eat you, frozen boots and all. Stop whining and crying." My encouragement had worn thin, as this was about the fiftieth time he had asked that question.

"I'll try," he wheezed, coughing.

"What would Little Joe do?" I asked.

Tear snot glazed his face, but my patience had diminished. I threatened to bury him in the snowdrifts as a frozen treat for desperate future travelers if he didn't stop whimpering in my ear. He nodded and we plodded forward; a Donner party of two.

We finally made it home (alive!) and my sister examined my feet. She said they were partially frostbit. I now have this story to relay to my kids when they complain about, well, anything.

"I walked five miles (I embellish a bit) in the snow with frostbitten toes!"

I did it though. I made it through, which actually placed a notch in my backbone. The Dad tally was down one.

*****

When the winter ice thaws from the bouldered, chunky mounds of dry sleepy ground, it drops like a fever with sweats and chills, and a kind of relaxed comfort settles into your bones. That is, until the flash floods re-carve the glacial caverns my motorcycle-laden sister would have to re-navigate. Subsequently she did, and the routine returned along with the odd brilliant drama of cactus flowers. Those flowers actually seem like an oxymoron to this arid country but there they were, fierce in color and shamefully lusty in fervor. They smack your senses as if to say, "You thought we couldn't grow here. Surprise!" I was shocked, every spring. I would continue to find my metaphor here, too.

The smell of rain as it hits the dry earth has become a standing metaphor as well, but to my soul. God, Heaven, and simply "being" was a sensual awakening to "a dry and weary land where there is no water." The scent is brisk, not like perfume or a good wine but more like morphine or a 20-year-old Russian vodka. It turns you into a hippie dancer at Woodstock. I never grew tired of the mornings at the ranch after such a spring rain.

I remember reading a story about a woman that lived in a dry desert-like area of Colorado. She was a gardener that had grown tired of the constant battle with the rigid land and was about to put her house up for sale. Then she expressed that, as she was at the end of her road, about to pound in the "For Sale" sign, it began to rain. She stopped and breathed in the pungent smack of earth and water and then heard the odd gurgling sound that occurred when this wetness seeped itself under the skin of the stubborn ground she wanted to leave. It became like the scorned lover; it was as if the land were boiling and its veins were filling with life, scent, and sound. She just couldn't leave.

Where else does the soil live out such a drama? Spring in the desert is all theatrics, wonder, and surprise. It was in this life-giving season that I found my swing.

LISA NORTH

Chapter 6: Swings and Soul Things

There are two types of people in this world: those that lived on swings at recess and those that kept their feet on the ground; those that savored flight and those that would rather walk, thank you very much.

Well, needless to say, I was the former.

I spent every recess on the swing set. I would dream and fly and write poems, thinking about the popular boy that normally didn't know I was alive, but actually was unaware of how desperately he loved me. All was soft, and the wind in my face was possibility.

Those dreams got me through the gruel of school. But as spring arrived, freedom became personified in every living thing. Summer was on the horizon, and life was full of promise and adventure.

One day, as I was out and about, exploring the new-found ground on the ranch's endless expanse again, I began to skip, full of joy at the actual colors that could follow such a season of so much stark and monotonous whiteness.

It wasn't until I reached a rapid, jaunty rhythm that I realized I had a companion—the kind of companion you might find in an Alfred Hitchcock movie. Jaunting behind me with rapid acceleration was a giant (at least, in rearview mirror vision) tarantula. They jump, you know—yep, like freakin' Olympic track stars. At that moment, my jaunt became a full-fledged sprint. I wasn't watching where I was heading, obviously, I was just trying to get away from the eight-legged serial killer. I had left the boundaries of our forty acres and was finally somewhere serial killers don't usually frequent—at least, not the eight-legged kind, mainly because they are not the "recess-swinger" types, thank goodness. Suddenly, right in front of me, hanging from an old oak tree, was the longest swing I had ever seen! It was like Grandpa himself had opened his arms and given me freedom.

It was tied to the highest and strongest branch on the tree—freedom and security, a marriage made in heaven—left here, for me, by a fellow recess comrade, no doubt. It would become my pendulum to Heaven where God and all the angels talk and sing together.

I climbed aboard and I was instantly transformed into the queen of the universe. Flights of fancy welled up into my bones. They were transformed into all hollowness, like those of larks and starlings. I would pump my legs and soar above the clumpy boulder line into the big blue and puffy white sky. Exhilarated and defiant, I would challenge all of my insecurities to defy this bliss.

When isolation and fear became my companions, that little sector on the outskirts of boundary lines would become my retreat; my private thinking, crying, and wishing place to go. I would find my solitude there, like my dad had found his on the edge of the porch where he would sit and look out into the evenings.

I would watch him as he stared out into the crags and clusters of the hillside, wanting in. I got it. He needed his recess, too. I think, for the longest time, he felt flight inside him, but he just didn't know how to stretch the boundary lines. That is, until he found his porch spot.

Later on, when life would flood his eyes and he would talk endlessly about God, finding your "Chi," and those stringy dimensions that lie beyond our finite notions, he began to sound an awful lot like a recess-swinger.

LISA NORTH

Chapter 7: Rodents Are Not Nice Bedfellows

After the spring rains, our little abode became a hostel to all the critters that wanted freedom and shelter from the torrential downpours that were flooding their natural homes. Their primary mode of transport was our bathtub. This tub was already a lovely shade of rust from the old iron-coated pipes, so it made a good camouflage for many creatures.

That first morning toilet visit was always a delightful surprise. Eyes sleep-crusted, all quiet except for the sound of the toilet tinkle and, of course, the rattle from the snake tail brazenly shaking up toward the hostile visitor; an alarm clock to beat all. But I began to grow used to our bathtub refugees. It was the guerilla warfare that occurred at nighttime that scared the bejesus out of me.

As we began to "rebuild and remodel" our ranch house, my bedroom became the worn-out, fungi-smelling couch in the living room, for quite a while longer than was promised.

It was the biggest room in the house, so I could have settled into my barracks just fine had it not been for the fact that it harbored the largest numbers of hostile enemies: mice— hundreds of them. At least, it seemed like hundreds, at night, when they would scurry about, in all formations, across the different routes of the floor. I would pull my blankets up to my chin and hope and pray they wouldn't take hostages. In the morning, I would find their special forces had left "special" droppings on my blankets! They had been there, right on top of me, while I slept! Ugh!

I recently read about how spiders find their ways into our open sleeping mouths during the night. We, supposedly, swallow upwards of four to five spiders a night. How did these researchers get their statistics? I mean, what sadistic scientist would sit and watch a sleeping person while spiders are climbing in and out of their mouths? Maybe the kind that might possibly also be able to determine just how many rodent CIA ninjas had climbed onto my blankets to scope me out?

You can imagine the horror and terror that accompanied my nights.

A few months ago, I met a young Lebanese man, serving at one of my favorite restaurants. He was a gregarious, jovial soul, and he began to tell us about growing up in Lebanon during the war. He said that all he remembered were the sounds of bombs going off outside his windows and how his father would bundle him and his sister up under their bed, completely surrounding them with pillows to cushion them from the horrors outside. This was his recollection of wartime, pillows, and comfort; a game of love.

I, however, was alone during my own personal war (okay, I admit, it was not quite the same thing, but follow me, here) under my blankets as spiders snuggled up on my tongue, no doubt, with green bereted rodents running amuck.

One night, the scurries were so bad, I decided it was time to make a run for it. I had already woken up around midnight to large droppings on my blankets. They were goliath-sized droppings, too, so we're either talking large mutant mice here, or rats! I didn't even want to think of that possibility!

I decided to go sleep in bed with my sister, but it was dark, black dark, and I had to bolt through enemy territory to get to her.

I held my breath and ran! I booked it into her room and climbed into bed with her. Lauren was "my pillows" and always had been—well, she and Grandma, but Grandma was not here. She, of course, let me climb into bed with her. I instantly relaxed and was in that sort of hazy as-you-drift-off kind of sleep where you can still see, blurrily, through your lids. What I saw, right smack in the center of my belly, sitting on his haunches, was an enormous rodent-like creature. I think it had fangs and ammo and it cussed like a middle-schooler. I screamed and popped him into the air. He scurried away, probably feeling terrified but also pretty proud of himself. He had a great story to tell his fellow comrades: "Got close to the enemy today… sat right on top of her, actually, and looked straight into her eyes…"

Up to that point, my sister had listened to my war stories, thinking they were a bit like fish stories, with ambivalence to the horrors I was facing nightly. Needless to say, I got a short night's sleep that night. The next day, I began to set traps. The war was on and I would fight back.

I'm not sure if I ever made much headway. Maybe I just got used to it all, like a good POW.

Chapter 8: Pacific Palisades Debutante

As I was struggling with my teenage metamorphosis, the image that stared back at me from the chipped, picture-frame-sized bathroom mirror wasn't exactly inspiring, Dad decided to marry Aphrodite. She possessed everything I didn't—lovely poise and a refined elegance. She was *practically perfect in every way*. Cecilia was her name and she had come to help run things on the ranch. Dad made quick decisions and before we could even really adjust to this new nymph in his life, she was his wife!

Cecilia was one of my dad's students when he was Dean of the law school in Los Angeles. Ten years his junior, she had latched on to his charms and he had comforted her during the sudden loss of her mother. All this made for the perfect match, right? Not quite, but we would get use to her, just like everything else. Or, at least, I would.

My sister never really did.

Lauren was my little brother's surrogate while Mom was on part-time hiatus. So, this chick was horning in on her territory. Besides, the new stepmom didn't have a clue about family life, raising kids, etc., but I could care less.

She was Beverly Hills beautiful and I wanted to be just like her. I realized I had already given this claim away to Mrs. Johnston, but that was then.

We didn't mourn her loss for very long and we had quick detachments to Dad's latent interests. I was ready to move on to my new, more refined move-in, and I was glad to have a bit of the city living here in our desert dwelling. Those expressions of "fish out of water" and "stood out like a sore thumb" had great significance for Cecilia.

When Mom remarried, we took a hike. We were shifted in the hierarchy, but Dad was different. He sort of treated his new wives or live-ins kind of like new pets. They were fun to have around, but not a distraction from us—his kin, his blood. (Blood is a big deal to the British.)

We tried our best to make her fit in. Actually, that's not true. We tried our best to make sure she could see that she didn't. It was pretty cruel, I guess. But it gave us the power we needed to maintain. My sister had, by necessity, become Derrick's mom. She watched over him, fussed over him, and basically covered him with her wings, making sure he had all that he needed, so that he wouldn't miss the one we left behind.

When this "pet" showed up as some kind of new mama bear to her little cub, a sabotage mission was put into place; covert, of course, but nevertheless palpable. "New Mommy" was not about to usurp Lauren's authority. Derrick and I followed suit.

Yet, I thought she was pretty wonderful. She was everything I aspired to be: beautiful and elegant, at all times, even in this stark, ridiculous setting. She had silk blouses that smelled like Saks Fifth Avenue perfume counters. She had her pants dry cleaned and they hung, perfectly pressed, on paper-covered hangers. Her hair was golden straight, with no puff ball in the back. She always slow-smiled, you know, the kind that feels gentle and slightly condescending; not quick, laughy, and cheerful ones, like mine and my mom's.

Nevertheless, she smiled often, spoke slowly, and moved gracefully across the cement floors. Her posture was like a dancer's and I always tried to hold myself like she did, even on the toilet! How she maintained such genteel composure in the chaos, I will never know. She moved like a gazelle. That is, until we made her feel like a deer in the headlights, on a daily basis.

What can I say? We were on a mission. She was getting in the way. Besides, we knew she was not long for the duration, so we were actually doing her a favor by speeding up the process.

When we were not ignoring her, we treated any of her attempts at connecting with us with just the slightest indifference. It was subtle—we didn't want Dad to completely catch on—and was just enough to be the catalyst for her isolation, so she would develop a female longing for companionship. Mission accomplished.

Sometimes, however, I would catch her looking out the window, and I would go stand near her, so she could feel some warmth... and so that I could, too.

I also had a window I looked out.

On one occasion, Dad was putting forth his effort for us all to get along and told us that Cecilia wanted to take us into the city (San Diego), for the day (lunch, shopping, and girl-stuff-plus-Derrick). It was one of those bored days where we were watching the tarantula wasps kill stuff, so we agreed to go with her. I sprayed my frizz ball down, put on my pink Dittos and favorite squirrel T-shirt, and we were off.

The day was fairly predictable. We lunched and shopped. I watched as Cecilia tried on the dresses from the mannequins and they wouldn't change. They'd look exactly like they did hanging on the plastic, posed women. She seemed to have the same blank expression when she tried them on, too. She moved in slow motion. As she noticed me watching her in awe, she smiled at me. I felt warm, and missed my mom. I wanted to feel close to Cecilia, but knew that it would deviate us from the mission, although I wasn't sure why we needed to sabotage her. To feel a little more alone? But Lauren was queen and we knew she was always right. I turned away from her smile.

As the day came to an end, we headed home. It was about a two-hour trek, and night was falling, solid and black, as nights in the desert do. Then it happened: the first thunder rumble.

There was no rain in sight, so we thought we knew what was coming, but we had no idea.

The rumbles began to get louder, and we noticed that we were the only ones on the road. Visions of disaster began to flash through our imaginations. Not fun. Just us, and our solitary little headlights punching holes into the zombie darkness. The thunder rolled across the landscape so loud that it seemed to make the road tremble, and maybe even a little girl with frizz-ball hair already standing up on the back of her neck.

"Hey, you guys, let's sing something." This was Cecilia's attempt at quieting our fears of lightning electrocution.

I was just glad we had tires. Of course, if a huge lightning bolt wanted to toast us, I'm sure four little rubber wheels were not much deflection.

"Ninety-nine bottles of beer on the wall," she began. "Ninety-nine bottles of beer. Take one down, pass it around, ninety-eight bottles of beer on the wall."

We held our defiance for a couple more beers on the wall, until the next roll of thunder.

"Ninety-five bottles of beer," I chimed in.

Lauren gave me a look of betrayal, but we might be on our way to the great beyond here and, by golly, I was going down with some beers off the wall.

Lauren held her defiant silence, until bottle 75. Pretty soon, there was a chorus of beers off the wall and even a laugh or two.

As we turned onto our exit, something astounding occurred. Like a flash from a camera that blinds you, the whole sky lit up for a second, flooded with lightning veins. It was an electrical storm like no other. Our bottles of beer were quieted, and we pulled off the road for a moment, just to watch the display.

We were silent in awe at this spectacle. We forgot to be afraid.

Cecilia reached for my hand. Her hand felt warm, like Mom's, but with no freckles, and it was soft, like a manicured flower. I wasn't sure who was comforting whom, but it didn't matter. Nature was being its fierce self and we were watching it together, all of us, huddled together, with only a few bottles of beer left on the wall.

*****

Being the notorious "ballplayer" he was, Dad began to want a new ballgame and Cecilia was starting to not be the player he wanted anymore. She would last a few years and pine for him much longer than that, but I began to see her slowly crumble. Her posture became like a tired dancer's droop. It was during that season that we had the accident.

Every now and then, we would take random treks into the city. Cecilia needed a dose of home. She was a city girl who needed a hit now and then. We typically went to just a larger town outside of our county. It was still adventurous for us, and close enough to the real thing for her, without being something achingly out of her reach.

Aside from the every-other-weekends with Mom, those trips were our big moment to connect with the real world. We would go into air-conditioned shops and watch Cecilia move like liquid through cashmere rounders. We would desperately try to pick up tips on how to look like real city dwellers when we got back to the cacti and Levi cut-offs.

One particular outing was different. I would remember it forever and flinch at the recollection.

Cecilia was distracted. The normal, gentle calm she possessed had jagged little edges that day. It wasn't until many months later that I would realize the deep rejection that had been festering just below the surface of her agitation. Dad was getting irritated by her, with her, and because of her. It was still in the subtle phases, yet kinesthetically palpable, nonetheless. The undercurrent was the kind that pulls you under and she was treading for dear life as fast as she could, just to appear to be above water. That day, however, she was sinking for minutes at a time before gasping a measly gulp of air.

Hence, the shopping spree.

We were just leaving the mall and all of us piled into her old green Pinto—not exactly like the Rolls and Jags she'd grown up with, but, hey, she was ranch-slumming now. Those little babies were better known as hatch-backed deathtraps.

I would later read up on the recalls of Pinto Hatchbacks due to something about the engine sitting somewhere near the hatch, apparently making it a fender-bender killer. This one was about to face up to that reputation. Although, lucky for us, it was a head-on collision. Phew!

Pintos are also a type of wild Indian pony. Little Joe (my David Cassidy) rode one, and I always wanted a Pinto horse. I would dream about owning my own horse for the next several years, but the closest I would get were two goats named Windsong and Nutmeg—don't be fooled by the cutesy names; mostly, they stunk.

Windsong developed a boil on the side of her cheek the size of a small child. It oozed on a continual basis. It was not exactly the equestrian scene I saw myself in, but I loved those old goats.

I'm diverting from my story.

Cecilia loaded us kids into the car. My brother, who preferred to stand up in the center of the car behind the gear shift (there were no seatbelts; this was '70s) and I were in the front passenger side of the car. My sister and our cousin were in the back. The light turned green—at least, Cecilia thought it did—and she proceeded to take a last gulp of air before treading into the intersection with her instant family.

The crunch of metal on metal is like fingernails on a chalkboard except the chalkboard is the inner lining of your nerves and the fingernails scrape and gnaw at them like a caged cat. The moment stays with you as though you pressed "replay" over and over, and it becomes the soundtrack for your life for a while.

The car was totaled. We were fortunate enough to not have been a part of that equation. I still, to this day, do not remember what my sister and cousin recounted to me as happening during the accident. I imagine it in slow motion, like in the movies, with some cool indie song playing in the background. I, supposedly, screamed as my little brother bounced off the gear shift and landed at my feet. This was after my forehead cracked the dashboard. (My dad always said I was "a hard-headed woman" and I would reply, in my best Cat Stevens rendition, "One who will make you do your best.")

I, apparently, did my best to survive a concussion to beat all concussions.

Cecilia had cracked the windshield with her head. Blood dripped down her porcelain skin. She ended up wearing a turban-like, gauze bandage contraption while the stitches healed, which gave her a more exotic, martyr-like persona.

What I do recall, however, when I finally "came to," was sitting on the bumper of the ambulance. I was there thinking, *Gee, do they not have a bed or a gurney or something for me? "Oh, let's just stick her on the bumper for a while. She and her throbbing, bulged-out forehead won't mind."*

I guess I was not damaged enough to make it into the actual ambulance—at least, not then, anyway. I managed to hitch a ride on a gurney to the hospital, eventually, but I think it was kind of an afterthought. Then, though, I was just grateful they didn't drive off with me and my concussion-welted face propped up against the brake lights.

My brother spent the night in the hospital. Derrick had a severely bruised spleen.

I was let out that day with the strict promise not to fall asleep too much or too often. That just meant more eating and TV-watching. Too bad we didn't own a TV.

When we returned in the morning, Mom was there. I held her (rather, she held me) for more time than hugs usually take. Her ruddy, tear-creased face looked like my grandma's whenever we would leave from a long visit. She would stand at the edge of her driveway, hold her face with one hand, and wave with the other, like a fragile flower vase about to topple.

Mom discovered that her baby boy had been asking for his mama throughout the night but she didn't even get the news about the accident until morning check-out time. Dad had sent in Cecilia. I don't think Mom ever forgave him for that.

There are a few desperate moments where we feel the need to enclose our children with nurturing, enveloping them like a cocoon, because we need the comfort as much as they do. It's like a mutual healing that needs to be totaled or summed. When the equation gets sent an outlier, the end result is a half-healing; a sort of continual gaping to the wound—like Windsong's boil, it just stays and oozes. I wanted to comfort my mom at that moment, and I wished I was injured a little worse so I could need her that way and she could complete her "mom circle."

I wanted to say, "Take me with you, Mom. We'll heal together. I don't mind playing second fiddle. By the way, no worries, she, the stepmom replacement, is on her way out."

And she was. Not long after the accident, there was another divorce. Lauren reclaimed her position and I went back to cut-offs, slumpy shoulders, and a new loneliness I didn't realize was there.

As Mom drove away, I stood on the hospital steps with my face and throbbing head in one hand, waving, like Grandma used to, with the other.

LISA NORTH

Chapter 9: Go-Carts, Coyotes, and Brothers

The cool thing about divorce is the guilt your parents feel. That was a scenario we knew how to navigate well. It meant that there was a slight break down in the parental pushback and we knew how to work it! I don't mean to sound jaded, but you get used to a rhythm of how things work. It becomes a kind of warped sense of normal. Divorce kids, especially if it is a recurring event, learn to hoard and grab attention and love… and sometimes a little bank!

Our divorce "settlement" for this particular go around was the way we kept ourselves in *Hostess Fruit Pies, Look Bars,* and *Pay Days*. We needed our sugar rations to survive the harsh deprivation (remember, we had no TV) and we devised an extortion plan. We were true financiers.

Here's how it worked. Every day or so, when my dad would lay out his coin change on the dresser, we would ask him if we could have it. He would agree to it every time, probably so he wouldn't have to weigh down his pockets with the cumbersome coin collection.

What he didn't realize is that we were Blackjack dealers, real sleight-of-hand swifties. We had a banking method: we would collect the change over the course of about a week, and then we'd casually ask him if we could exchange the change for bills. He fell for it every time. This was better than getting an allowance because it was a game, too!

Looking back now, I realize there wasn't much that could get past Dad's razor-sharp legal mind. He was onto us but played along. I think that he was simply being led around by his guilt.

His remorse didn't last too long, but we usually got some cool stuff in the interim. On one such occasion, after a visit with Mom, when he saw second thoughts in my eyes, I landed myself a go-cart.

Lauren was the official owner of the Honda 150 that was our morning mode of travel to the bus stop. I guess Dad could also see that I was really the one that lamented Cecilia's absence the most, so the go-cart was all mine! (Derrick was too young to remember all the trauma, so a new cap gun sufficed for him.)

Imagine a little ground-hugging roadster, like a miniature dune buggy and the rocky dunes became my escape. I was free fallin' like Tom Petty all the time, and all over the forty acres.

One day, I decided to extend my generous condescension to my little brother.

He looked especially needy that day as he smacked all the Yucca plants and watched the battered milkweeds bleed. Even our bloodhound, Baskerville, with his normal resiliency to Derrick's tirades, avoided the little two-foot ranter, so I offered him a ride.

The day was filled with sunshine and I was filled with a little mischief and flight. I normally stayed on the dirt roads that bordered our homeland, within eyeshot of Dad—if he was looking—or our neighbors, our only neighbors, Al and Margie. Al was a retired sergeant from the army and Margie was his desert bloom (more about them later).

That particular day, I decided Derrick and I would Lewis-and-Clark it. He was game, tired of hitting the dog and digging for arrowheads, of which we had dozens already. I informed him over the roar of the metal-framed contraption that we were going to off-road it for a while.

I think he agreed, but off-roading that low to the road is a bit like being dragged behind a horse because you feel all the bumps and hear all the rocks and cactus crunches. We were on our way somewhere foreign and mysterious. To heck with maps and rules and playing it safe!

Maybe I felt braver because I wasn't alone; my kin was with me, the flesh of my flesh. I could press on to new heights with my blood around me, even if the blood was only four years old and about forty pounds of extra weight. Pretty soon, the house was out of sight, as were Al and Margie's sprinklers.

This all would have been just grand, had we not run out of gas.

At the slow puttering out of the engine, there was a moment of just sitting in our seats with the desert silence before I stated the obvious,

"You forgot to remind me to fill up the tank."

"Huh?" he sputtered.

"Yup, you forgot. It was my job to drive and take you on this incredible journey. All you had to do was remember the gas. That's it!" I belabored.

I continued, "You know what? Forget it. I know where we are. I just need to get us back on the road. Don't think I'm going to carry you, either!" I kept on for a while until I noticed he was unresponsive.

Normally, this would be about the time he would start to cry. My little brother was not a wuss, by any means—he would tackle tick-laden hounds and swat at tarantula wasps—but, for some reason, excursions with me didn't end very well. He was probably having snowdrift memories, right about then. But it was at that moment that he shut up entirely. I observed his eyes widen and his jaw open, drool-lipped and stationary. His body went limp. I turned to see what he was staring at—or, rather, what was staring back at him.

There's a quiet strength to desert creatures. They possess a warrior-like stillness steeped in restful acceptance, accompanied by a censorship that is both sweet and terrifying, more deafening than your own internal voice that pierces the mind's eye. Still, I gathered my inner voice to reason with myself that coyotes are pack animals.

This ominous creature was both sleek and scrawny. His fur was a grayish tan, much like the weeds and grasses that were his living room. He was six feet away from us and all alone, which dictated my next set of thoughts; panicked thoughts that spilled over one another.

I'll bang on something loud. I don't know what, yet, but something. Or I'll hold Derrick on my shoulders and wave his hands around so we look bigger. Hopefully, the coyote won't decide to howl for his kin to come join in a meal.

Yet, I just sat there, hypnotized. We all did, alone in our own moment. We stared at each other for what seemed like a lifetime before the animal gently padded off, leaving no sound but my own thoughts. He and I we were the same; loners, off from our packs, finding our own way, trying desperately to define ourselves by our surroundings.

Derrick and I made it home in two pieces. It was a long walk, pulling the go-cart behind me, straddled by a cowboy.

Needless to say, the next time I offered Derrick to come with me on a reckless adventure, he respectfully declined.

Chapter 10: White Bull Named Dennis

The next adventure I remember is the story I tell my kids when the power goes out, or as we sit around a campfire. It's also the one they recount in family reports for school or in recess discussions, in the "my dad can beat up your dad" kinds of scenarios, except this was about their mom, when she beat up a bull the size of a bulldozer. Well, sort of.

*****

Dad had an old, paint-peeling pick-up truck that served as our hauler. It hauled everything from wood to illegal construction workers (a later story).

*****

I have since tried to find a beat-up old pick-up with just the right amount of paint peel, so the rusty scratches show through the dents, and with just the right color of powdery, pale bluish primer that is reminiscent of country songs and road trips.

*****

On many an occasion, I would hop in the back of Dad's pickup for outings to the General Store, the dump, or to get dog food or whatever else we needed. It was an expedition, a way to break up the monotony or the heat.

One occasion, however, involved none of those reasons just recounted but, rather, a death-defying act of reckless abandonment.

There was a white, Indian-owned wild bull the locals and natives named Dennis. He was the neighborhood menace. Right off, you understand the correlation to the comic strip icon that possessed pointy, blond hair.

Dennis had become a half-legend to us, I say "half" because we thought we saw him one day amongst the other wild bulls who roamed freely and grazed on the land. (The Federal government allotted free reign of the land to the Indians for the purpose of grazing their cattle.) This made for interesting walks home from the bus stop when Lauren started high school and was no longer my biker companion.

Dennis was real, and he was, in fact, a menace.

He ripped through fences, trampled people's gardens, and basically wreaked havoc wherever he went.

At least, this was what everyone claimed. We were not sure we believed it all until the day when Dennis showed up out in the field behind our house.

He was a twelve-foot, horned monster of a beast, chomping on milkweed, no doubt.

There was an understanding (or so I imagined) amongst all the neighbors of the territory that "he who captured the big, white, monster bull would be honored with a large-feather headdress and the respect of all the reservation." At the very least, it would be a feather in the cap of whoever was able to corral this creature and keep him constrained against fences and gardens.

There he was, and there was Dad, loading himself into the pick-up.

I had presumed that he was making his usual jaunt to the store. I was, unfortunately, horribly off in my presumption.

I think I yelled something like, "Hey, Dad, can I come?"

He yelled back something like, "You sure you want to?"

So, I jumped into the back and awaited the bumpy ride to the store. But he had a little detour in mind first. He headed out onto the road for a few dozen yards, then he hauled it full speed out into the field, where *Dennis the Menace* was free-roaming.

I've often watched the bull chases in Spain on TV and rodeo clowns that get flipped into the air like juggling balls and thought, *I, too, know the fury of "bull," in all its many colors and situations.*

This one, in particular, was like facing a nemesis. I bounced and flailed about the rust and primer, making dents of my own. Beside me, the nostrils of a frightened beast were flaring as he snorted. His horns scraped the sides of the truck. His eyes were wild and frenzied. They locked with mine.

In that instant, we both knew that one pothole or popped tire would be all it would take to make me his next fence or garden.

My dad had his lasso out and my hippie cousin, Dan, was in the next seat, long hair waving and mustache stretched as he grinned from ear to ear at the hilarity of my situation.

Dennis outran them, eliciting the age-old postulate that, in fact, the survival impulse does actually trump the self-actualizing momentary triumph of man over beast.

I was dizzy and had bruises and ringing ears. My dad, however, found the incident hilarious. He chuckled as he asked me if I still wanted to come with him to the store.

"No, thanks. You go. Catch ya next time," I said, limping out the back end.

"You bet," he said, "Hey, you're a good sport, daughter of mine!"

That was much praise. To fight the good fight in any and all situations was always what he expected, and consequently, deserved the highest of praise.

My dad was not the kind of guy to wave banners or hand out cigars to the winner of anything. Rather, he appreciated you putting forward all your guts for display, even if they got trampled on, literally. It's the "last guy standing" philosophy he appreciated—not the last guy with the medal around his neck or the last team number on the scoreboard. In fact, he wasn't much into scoreboards. He was all about the ring; the boxing ring was his passion. He was a boxer in school and would have had a full boxing scholarship had he stayed in the motherland.

Nevertheless, this fist-to-fist, man-to-man passion was passed down to us. When other good American families were huddled around the "telly" for the Super Bowl, we were ringside, watching Muhammed Ali take on his next brazen counterpart. I saw every Muhammed Ali fight there ever was and could spew out all knowledge of what makes for a great boxing match. That knowledge did not come in very handy, as I had three girls who would have rather had their mother slightly more abreast on what "off-sides" means while a ball is flying or going foul or something like that. But the rules of the match taught me valuable life lessons, such as to remain in the game until you fall, to fight until you can't lift your arms anymore, to not hit below the belt, and to know what you're up against; know your opponent. In this case, it was just a frightened beast out for a little midday snack of milkweeds who was suddenly faced with his own mortality.

One thing I learned from watching the nuances of the ring was that when fear locks eyes with you, even if it is only for a split second, it can be a moment of standoff.

Perhaps that's why the chase ended and the beast was released. Could it be that Dad, in the rearview mirror, caught that interlocking and the brakes took the next moment to a halt? Perhaps the umpire decided to ring the bell and call this round a tie.

I remained standing, arms still able to throw a punch if needed. My belt was still buckled firmly around my cut-offs. For that, apparently, I garnered a bit of the umpire's respect. It was worth all the paint bruises and rust-encrusted lumps.

Dennis would resurface, every now and then, but there was an understanding, of sorts; a standoff. My dad would glare at him from his porched throne and Dennis would strike the ground with his hoof, breathing steam, then nod and head off down the road to someone else's fences and fields. The ring cleared and the crowd dispersed. The match was over… until the next fight.

Chapter 11: Hippie Cousins, Barn Life, and Porch Shrines

Inevitably, when someone catches a falling star and puts it in their pocket, the itch becomes contagious and people (i.e. cousins) come out of the woodwork to see if all the crazy hoopla is for real. "Show us that damn star in your pocket, Mister." Pretty soon, they want a little piece of the action.

Not long after we got settled into our cabin, our cousins decided that our place was the new commune.

They were on their way to "Woodstock." Apparently, it must have been overcrowded, so they decided to plant "roots" in our backyard, so to speak.

They were good with woodwork and, even though we didn't quite have a working bathroom yet, Dad began to get the commune fever himself. He would always talk about families that lived together all under the same roof, sharing chores, meals, and bathrooms.

The problem was that we didn't yet have a full working roof, and our single bathroom was always a work in progress. Sometimes the waiting line was singular, if the bathtub had to be cleared of its latest catch, or if the toilet had to simply rally up enough gumption to flush itself.

We had plenty of chores, and meals were usually pretty interesting. Each of us was responsible for at least one dinner during the week. The menu didn't change much. I knew how to make one thing: tacos, every week. Lauren could change it up a bit, but she was big on omelets. Dad had his version of some kind of borscht. It wasn't exactly a British thing, now that I think about it, although he claimed it was British, stick-to-your-guts-in-the-war-trenches kind of food. It was pretty great and it did stick with me; the warmth and calming effect could shut out the grit and grime of a day's work.

There was also always some version of British fare fitting in somewhere, though, such as chip sandwiches, the kind of thing that could elicit a heart attack just looking at it, but it was a great midday snack for us. Basically, it consisted of large, wedged, French fries, white bread, and butter. Every good Brit has a chip pan. This pan is passed down from generation to generation. I believe ours came from an Old Saxon who lived in the deserted outskirts of Stonehenge. Oil and all came with it, but damn if it didn't make a "grrrrand" pot full of chips. I'm not sure where the pan is today; it's probably tucked in a cupboard somewhere, waiting for its rightful heirs to claim it.

All of this fit into Dad's grand scheme—a sense of place with kin all around, and meals with desert quiet and civilization at bay. A commune likened to the word itself, everyone communing to the sounds of nature's rhythms and chip sandwiches. My hippie cousins were down with that karma.

The only glitch, and I'm not quite sure they knew this when they packed up the van, but Roof Number One was full, so they would be displaced to seek refuge in our dilapidated, should-be-condemned barn. Winters would be memorable, like Shakespeare and his discontent, only with a little comical disaster thrown in for laughs. They seemed happy to have it, though, and they moved in to the back-corner section, the less dilapidated section. It was an odd sensation to walk up there. To look from the outside, it was like it was out of an old western movie where the cowboys slowly got off their horses because surely nobody could be living in such a broken-down piece of crap, yet there was a disconcerting stir of life coming from the less dilapidated corner in the back.

"Hold yer fire, boys. Let's take a look inside, slowly now, slowly," I could hear the voice of my inner commentary say.

Somehow, I would find a way to maneuver past the falling, broken bowels of the abode until I reached the little apartment section. It, surprisingly, ended up having a kind of charm, like a fort with blankets. They lived there longer than I lived on the ranch, I think, through several winters and a baby. They named her with a spring month and the word for morning in the middle. I'm sure spring had deep meaning for them, as did making it through another night, until morning dawned again.

My cousin, Christina, was beautiful in her prime; I use to think she was so hip. She was always bangled, smelled like sandalwood, wore long tapestry skirts, and had a fun grin. It was odd, though, for me, the first time I caught sight of her armpits. She had this rich, brown cascade of hair that, I was convinced, she could pull just behind her ears. I always thought she looked like Natalie Wood (I watched too many of those tear-jerker movies) but there was a sweet, woeful anguish to her resiliency. Nonetheless, when I saw that same cascade of rich locks coming from her armpits, I have to say, it mesmerized me. I could watch her move around in her summer tank tops for hours as I thought of ways to braid it, style it, or just comb it. That cinched it for me, though. All that hippie stuff, in theory, sounded great—peace and love, etc.—but they forgot to throw in the furry armpits. I didn't sign up for that!

Come to think of it, long hair was critical to hippie-ness. My cousin's husband, Dan, had hair exuding from every orifice. I think he may have even had hair coming out his ears, literally. He was weirdly clean-chested, though.

Nevertheless, we would get use to our new communers because they were now a part of the construction team: Dad, two barely teen girls, a four-year-old cowboy, sometimes a debutante wife (Cecilia still lingered for a while after the divorce, and then, later on, there was a live-in named Lydia), and pregnant hippie cousins with hair. This was going to be one hell of a house/commune.

Construction was about to under way, but first things first. We were to start with the redwood front porch. I thought this was an odd starting point, given that we didn't exactly have a working bathroom and I was still sleeping on the couch in the living room, but sometimes the artistic imperative for expression simply takes over pragmatism.

Dad decided to make the outside of our house a sort of shrine filled with symbolism. It was to be a montage of words and totems, with life's hidden meanings carved into the railings and banisters. They were to be burned into the redwood as a testament to the regard we shared for the Native land, as a sort of alms to the sacred desert air, and just really deep, hippie stuff like that.

I'm still not sure what all of it meant, but, nevertheless, we were tasked with shellacking and varnishing the symbols that were carved and burned into the rust colored wood by Cousin Dan, Christina's husband, AKA Barn Resident. He resembled one of the ZZ Top guys if they had not eaten for a few weeks. He had doleful eyes and an artistic sensibility when he wasn't slightly stoned. "Slightly" is within functional limitations and gives a heightened sense of the world. Dan was also a philosopher, but he had some skills.

Before the bedrooms were finished, before the kitchen got started, and before the "Shangri-La" bathroom was conceived, the most important construct of all was delegated: the wraparound porch. This porch would become my dad's throne; his monastery. So, it was fitting that it would have to be shrine-like in design.

Dan was the artisan and we were the laborers. The whole porch would be carved out of redwood, because redwoods are majestic. They personified something eternal that lasts beyond us, and so they did. (On my return to the ranch, the day we laid out my dad's ashes, that porch was still standing, with all of the symbols and carvings, scuffed up by time and weather. Nevertheless, the symbols still mysteriously held a secret code of meaning that embellished that sacred porch. They spoke of something deep and permanent to my dad, and are still there, speaking. Over the door was the symbol of a bird. It was like an emblem and included our surname, a claim we would make permanent by the ash to dust of that day.)

Dan began to carve away. There would be images and symbols carved, then burned black, for effect. It was gorgeous, which felt odd, juxtaposed against the ugliness of everything else. There were symbols of Latin words for peace and love, Yin Yang exposés, and even Jesus was thrown into the mix.

"It's a testament to revelations throughout history and it's like the cliff writings of the Indians, like on the boulder clumps," Dad explained.

He would stand back and observe his monastery cliff-dwelling, eager to find his solace. He and Dan would spend their evenings drinking *Dos Equis* and mapping these carvings out for the next day as we, the laborers (my sister, brother, and I), would try to wash all of the sticky varnish out of our hair, fingers, and ears.

The varnish was everywhere! We were stuck, like permanent super glue, because we had the commission to varnish and shellac these "cliff drawings" of redwood, over and over, day in and day out, applying several coats, until the porch shined like the Mexican coffee tables we remembered from our occasional treks to Tijuana.

The porch was a cross between something ethereal that should be draped with prayer flags at the top of a mountain and something you'd find at a national park gift shop. That is, until it would rain buckets (monsoons often accompany summers in the desert), then it would look like a horrible sunburn that peels, causing chunks of flesh to fall off. When that happened, we would resume our positions and varnish again.

It was about six months before all of the varnish left my hair; it gave a new definition to "sculpting hair gel."

I started to feel like those bugs preserved in chunks of amber, stuck in a yellowish crust for life. No matter how many baths or showers I took, I was varnish crust. Somehow, though, it felt important to me—symbols and words carved into wood, and shellacked to my soul.

My identity was indelibly linked to the red trees and weathered railings that would outlast us. It was another root-digging, place-embedding way to be in this crazy commune and maybe even feel a little peace and what smelled like love. Or maybe it was just the perpetual waft of green smoke coming from the barn at all moments of the day. Hippies!

Chapter 12: Neighbors and Distant Relatives

I'm not sure what it is that makes us feel safe, either in a place or in our own skin. Deep, shared intimacies provide that feeling, like "pillows and comforters." Sometimes, it's just a sense of being and how you can simply and holistically "be" with certain people. It's like your mom's hand on your fevered forehead. You can fall asleep without risk of drifting away, because the power of Mom's healing hands keep you safe; like a magnetic force field of compassion.

There were way too many lonely moments to recount in that desert sanctuary. The silence could be deafening, as could my own thoughts. I liked the feeling of being frozen in a tunnel with sound, life, and walls at bay, but sometimes it just freaked me out. Isolation can be super cool when you're in mid-life and done with some of the corrupting elements of the outside world, but when you're a twelve-year-old, it can kind of make you think you're in a *Twilight Zone* episode.

Our neighbors to the north, however, Al and Margie, kept the compass from spinning and the fifth dimension from closing in too frequently. They were a delightful, retired couple from somewhere around the east coast or the San Diego area. Al was a military sergeant who always looked as if he had just come home from the war and was able to get only his coat off—the fatigues and boots stayed on. I thought his cropped hair looked like one of those perfect lawns that gets mowed four or five times a day, except his lawn was silver. He had a gruff, sergeant voice and told loud stories, full of anecdotes, that I'm sure were the PG versions, censored for our ears.

Margie was a glorious china doll, perfect and lovingly weathered by the harshness of her residence, not by life or despair. She was his antithesis. With bourbon-colored hair and florals about her trim figure, she would sit like a ballet dancer while his stories flew around the room, her eyes never leaving him.

They had all the dangling noises, bells, and chimes that make a home feel like an ashram and theirs was a real home with kitchen plaques on their walls that said things like, "If Mama ain't happy, ain't nobody eatin' tonight!"

Even though she had the poise and etiquette of an elegant lady, she had a little spice in her kitchen.

Otherwise, I suppose, she couldn't have weathered the sergeant for all those years.

Sitting in their whimsical living room with a cup of tea lovingly prepared by Margie's delicate, china doll hands gave me that little sense of security I didn't even know I was missing.

Sometimes, I would lie in bed at night, unable to sleep, and I would look up the hill and see Margie's lights on. She was a bit of a night owl. Maybe that was her time to find her own sense of safety and space, connecting with the nocturnes that prefer the cool, stark blackness. I would think, *Maybe Margie is setting her hair right now in little pink curlers, like my grandma does every night.* Then I would think of my grandma, her soft baby hair, and the gnarled, veined hands that held mine, and I would think of Margie's, crafted with age and gardening begonias, yet still manicured perfectly. *Maybe she is drinking a cup of chamomile from a china cup on a lace doily,* I would muse, *settling her own world down gently.*

Margie never knew that just her light being on would settle mine, like healing hands on a fevered brow.

LISA NORTH

Chapter 13: Indian Relics and Haunted Shacks

I had always maintained a humble awareness that the ground we walked upon was a bit hallowed. It had once been trodden by the Native dwellers that were displaced to the reservation just over the hill. I had a respect and maybe even a bit of guilt over this fact. I was, in fact, a trespasser. But I also had a reverence for the dirt below my feet.

On lonely, dust-kicking days, I would imagine there had been revolutions or battles or, at least, a cowboy and Indian western movie that had played out on the tumbleweed-filled fields.

There was a cluster of boulders that sat high up on the hill, just beyond where the road ended. This was the landscape my dad would sit and stare off into, from his porch deck chair.

To me, it was like my very own personal archeological site. Lauren, Derrick, and I would climb through the boulders, always checking the snake holes for rattlers, of course, of which we had many. Some people around these parts cook up their rattlers and eat 'em. ("They taste like steak!") I prefer chicken, thank you very much.

It was on one of our various expeditions that we discovered a little Indian "kitchen." There were carved bowl shapes in the rocks where the Indians would grind their corn, and we found actual granite grinders as well as countless arrowheads. Yes, it was official; we were trespassers on ground we did not belong to, nor earn. Our neighbors dwelled in the clumps of government housing over the hill, while we explored their heritage in a mound of kitchen boulders. Nevertheless, we claimed this little kitchen clump as our new fort. We would play out domestic scenarios there, in some way, and try to connect to the population just over our hill and in our classrooms.

I had a friend named Georgia who lived on the Rez. She let me borrow her brush once, and I brought home lice (that was fun) but we stayed friends anyway, though I used my own brush from that point on. She had long black hair, smiley eyes, and a big laugh. Everyone liked Georgia.

One day, I asked her what she wanted to be when she grew up.

I said, "I think I want to be an actress, or maybe a dolphin trainer—or maybe a model, if I get this tooth fixed in front. See?" I showed her my crooked front tooth that I would always be slightly embarrassed by, and she laughed her big laugh. Then she drifted off, in contemplation. She mulled over my question for a while and held a desperation in her eyes I hadn't seen on smiley Georgia before.

Then she simply said, "To get off the reservation."

I hope she is running free somewhere, maybe near big, open spaces, with boulder clusters of opportunities, and off the Rez.

*****

As all great explorers will tell you, on any significant expedition into the unknown, one is bound to come across something haunted. It's just what happens—at least, when you are under the age of reason, which allows imaginations to skip and jump with wild abandon.

One lazy, sleepy day, like the type where you watch tenacious little ants carry stuff or throw random objects for the dogs to retrieve, Dad, noticing our boredom, told us to "go take a hike."

I'm not sure he meant this literally, but we decided it wasn't a half bad idea, so we did.

We actually had our bikes, so, you know, we were kind of invincible. Bike air, I am convinced, creates such invincibility it must contain drugs or something; laughing gas, maybe. So, we took a mountain bike hike, which made us feel pretty badass. We raced down the dirt roads until we reached a hill we had not climbed up before. Unexplored territory! We looked up the hill for a while, strategizing our trail choices. Then Lauren just started plowing ahead and up—fearless, of course.

She yelled, "Come on! This is cool!"

Naturally, I had to comply, because to stay down below, where cowards hold their tails, by myself, was not an option.

We weed-whacked our way through and up the hill until we finally reached an old abandoned shack with rock-blasted windows and tar-papered walls.

We both just stood still for a while. Creepy tingles settled into our flesh. Cobwebs hung from the old, sun-faded curtains, which were slightly pulled back, as if knobby, bony fingers held them back.

Suddenly, the whole area seemed to be transfixed into a zombie-like, apocalyptic scene and I thought, *Hey, I don't think dead people appreciate unannounced visitors.* Then it occurred to me that, maybe, they actually really like it. Hence, I began to plot my escape route.

Then Lauren said, "Let's go in."

Are you freakin' kidding me? No way! In my mind's eye, I was already bolting down the hill, leaving her to fend for herself with the flesh-eaters, but I said, "Okay. You first."

She bravely walked up to the door.

I took one baby step closer. It was silent; sinister silent, like in those movies where you're screaming at the screen to the moronic characters that should obviously know they are dead meat, but instead decide to drink copious amounts of alcohol and camp out for the night, when you, the omniscient audience, know the ax-swinging, patchy-fleshed maniac is just around the next.

The silence was broken by a crackling in the cacti. It was enough to send Lauren bolting out past me. Past me!

Immediately, I was on her trail, wheeling over dried sage clumps and crackling, thorny weed bushes, sucking up our bike drugs, pedaling furiously. We were down in record time. We felt triumphant, as though we had come and conquered. Conquered what, I'm not sure, but something inside. We had touched *Boo Radley's* door, and lived to tell the tale. Ahh, exploration!

We later found out that someone had actually been killed, or died, or was murdered—something like that—in the old abandoned shack that haunted our dreams for a while. But we had a story to embellish at school the next week, so it was all good. We had bit off a small chunk of the fears we coddle and lived past, and through, them.

Eleanor Roosevelt said, "Do something you're afraid of every day."

I guess baby steps of fear-conquering might actually be the stuff of true explorers.

Chapter 14: Goats, Gottingers, and Butchered Pigs

The great and not-so-wonderful part of living on a 40-acre spread in the middle of Nowhere-land, living as a Nowhere-man (or girl), is that a "body" can get just a tad bit lonesome. I had my siblings, of course, but sometimes you just get tired of runt cowboys and slightly bossy sisters! So, naturally, I was elated when I discovered that just a mere half-mile away lived my new best bud, Ellen Gottinger.

Ellen's family were goat farmers. In fact, they had goat everything! I am convinced that Ellen's mom made the first known goat cheese. She made everything out of goat milk.

When I met her mom for the first time, she asked me if I would like some goat cookies with a nice cold glass of goat's milk. As I turned toward her, it dawned on me that her nose—and Ellen's nose, for that matter—looked familiar, kind of like how people resemble the dogs they have as pets, you know, like the long-haired, scruffy, old hippie chick with the Afghan Hound, or the short, stocky guy with chubby, ruddy cheeks and stubby nose with the bulldog. The Gottingers looked like their herd! Their noses moved when they talked, just like their progenies. I was mesmerized by their talking noses. I half-expected a "baa" when they laughed. But I thought it was all just perfect! My best bud had a goat farm and I got to go over there all the time to milk the goats, which I did, on a regular basis.

One day, Ellen called me and asked, "Hey, you want to come over? We'll milk the goats and then my dad is gonna butcher the pig! You want to help?"

I looked around. Derrick was naked except for his cowboy hat and boots, oh, and vest, of course, and was beating the dog (his horse) with a stick. I decided, if I stayed home, I would just taunt him until he cried; not a good option. Lauren was in the barn with our hippie cousins. Hmmm.

"Yup, I'm in. Sounds fun! I'll be there in 20!"

There is something austere and poetic about a disemboweled pig. At least, that's what I kept telling myself for the weeks and months afterward, when I had nightmares about Ellen's "Wilbur," hanging up by his toes, to bleed, while we milked the goats.

Farm kids must have the backstage pass to life. They knew what the meat in those nice, little

Styrofoam, plastic-wrapped packages actually had to endure to make it into them. They remembered when the little, plucky-feathered fowls would run free, pecking the ground, before their necks got rung. Actually, they still run around after their necks are rung. I better stop or I may become a Pescatarian!

The day started out great. Ellen and I got into our ritual of goat milk fights in between filling buckets full of something that resembled milk. I didn't consider goat milk real milk; it came out warm and smelled like sour mold. We squirted each other from head to toe with the gamey, sticky, white body fluids that flowed out the teats of the mama goats. There's nothing like a goat milk fight in an old musty barn with your best friend.

However, the day was about to take a turn.

I stepped through the goat pen opening to empty my bucket into the containers when I saw Ellen's dad heading toward the pig pen with a large carving blade in his hand. I froze. He grabbed a fat one and walked him out to the hose, then washed him up, nice and pink. I had just read *Charlotte's Web* the year before, and the story flashed through my sensibilities. Dread settled in the pit of my stomach and I began to bite my fingernails; a habit I still find useful in stressful situations. I guess, somehow, I knew what was coming, but my senses were still awash with farm-life fun!

When he took out his knife and slit the pig's throat, I felt as if the blood left my own face, and I felt a tingly, dark tunnel close me in. I took a breath, knowing that I might faint right there in the goat pen, just like Wilbur.

As I stood in the barn doorway, soaked in the goat milk steaming off my shirt, the rancid scent of milk and sweat filled my nose. I stared at the bleeding pig. I think a piece of innocence left me at that moment.

So, this is how life works, huh?

I immediately envisioned all of the people in the world, stripped of their dignity. They say that with struggle comes compassion, except for the powerless, that is; indignancy trapped in hands tied—or hooves, in this matter. Death, to me, became a bloody, hanging mess. I could smell the metallic scent of it fill the air, and I just stood there, unable to move.

Slowly, I was shaken out of my stupor by Ellen's dad, shouting, "Hey you two, come watch. I need you to empty the intestines!"

I thought I was hearing things.

Drunk with anxiety, I said to Ellen, "Did your dad just tell us to watch out for tempting decisions?" I was, apparently, still in my deep, philosophical death analysis.

Ellen giggled; I think there was a slight "baa" in there.

"He wants us to clean out the pig intestines. He's gonna smoke 'em! You guys can have some. They're really good."

I thought I might puke. I had visions of smoking pig intestines, like cigarettes, and then gobbling them up.

"Oh, that's okay. I'll just watch." I thought that was the best I could do. In fact, just watching felt like climbing a mountain, at that very moment.

Ellen said, "No. Come on! It's fun!"

Fun? I suddenly felt sorry for my poor, sheltered, goat-infested friend. She needed to get out more; go to Disneyland or a skating rink or something. I wanted to tell her that intestine-squeezing is not exactly on the Condé Nast Traveler list of top ten activities to do and see in the world. Instead, as though spoken in a tunnel, I heard the words come out of my mouth.

"Okay. Sounds fun."

Then my feet were walking over to the hanging, skinned pig. His fat was rippled and in white lumpy pockets, like a bed full of old pillows, yet he was stiff. His snout faced the ground and his gut was completely opened up.

At that moment, the PTSD was pushed aside and I went into focus mode. I was simply in biology class, yes, that's it, with Mrs. Johnston; of course, Mrs. Johnston. She would get a kick out of this. Ellen's dad, in his bloody overalls, was carving away. Sweat and little flakes of pig fat were stuck in his mustache. I felt dizzy again.

"Hold it together!" I told myself and took a few deep breaths. He handed me the pig bowels.

"Here you go. Just go squeeze these puppies clean as a whistle!"

Puppies? Whistles? Pig fat mustache! I puked. Ellen laughed; baa, baa. I asked to go home—after the bowels were squeezed clean, of course.

Ellen's mom called from the kitchen, "Lunch time! Bacon and goat cheese sandwiches!" At least, that's what I heard. I said my dad was expecting me home. I washed my hands, five times, and ran through the field, back to the warmth of my adobe block and the naked cowboy.

I skipped lunch that day.

After dinner, my dad said, "Mrs. Gottinger brought dessert over for us—goat cheese cake!"

I ask to be excused and retired to bed early, only to dream of pig intestines and goat… everything.

Chapter 15: Pets, Sort Of

Animals possess a tempering quality. They lift us out of the neurosis that is humanity and spread us out into the leaves, trees, and the landscapes outside of us… most of the time. More often than not, however, they just become cleanup projects; sweaty, furry creatures who wear their disgustingness for all to see. They share our living space yet, somehow, creep into our beings and settle there. Even though we ask them to move over, they stay… and we don't even realize we need them.

We decided, after our Gottinger encounters, that we would build a goat shed and fill it with our own milk-squirters. Back when this whole ranch proposition had initially been considered, a horse was on the list of promises. I had visions of a horse ranch, for a while, but those were soon displaced by the reality of goats as the next best thing. At least, that's what Dad propagated.

*****

Thinking back, the weekend before Mom's wedding, we were sitting outside Dad's Malibu trailer.

That was his newest temporary dwelling, on a cliffside, overlooking the star-dotted coastline. It lasted a couple of months, which was a little long for a camping trip, but we got to camp with him, every other weekend, and discuss this new life adventure.

"So, what do you think? Are you guys in?" Dad laid out the plan for the ranch, and I was trying to place myself there; see it.

"Can I get a horse?" This was the deal-cincher, for me to be able to leave Mom.

"I don't see why not. There's a barn and we can fix it up! In fact, that will be a great project for all of us!" he promised.

Dad's enthusiasm was contagious, sort of like a flu you can't shake. Little did I know that this "project" would not only be pervasive to the whole picture, but my horse would soon become goats with boils on their cheeks and hippie cousins would cohabitate in the barn rather than my Palomino named "Honey."

*****

Our dilapidated barn held not only our cousins, but an occasional, illegal Mexican immigrant (a later story), so, no room for a horse. I guess my dad had a bit of guilt over the horse promises that were dashed, so he built a little goat shed a bit of a walk away from the house and we got two goats, a mom and a baby—Nubians to be exact, but I just called them the "floppy-eared" kind. I got to name them: Windsong and Nutmeg. They would hunker down through harsh winters and, eventually, Windsong's face would swell with a boil the size of a grapefruit on her cheek. But I still thought she was lovely. Unfortunately, they slowly disappeared from my priorities as I began to be more interested in my go-cart and the other self-indulgences I would carve out for myself in order to survive. I can still see their sad, little, shed faces, baa-ing away for me, hoping I remembered to feed them and maybe, just once, to scratch their heads to let them know I was aware they existed.

Goats were on the periphery, but what we needed in order to really thrive in the tumult of a desert existence was a good dog. That would really help with the forgotten horse promise.

Dad grew up a reader. He read more books than any living being I ever encountered. In fact, they were companions to him. He felt more at home inside a book than any three-dimensional setting. So, it made sense that our dog would have to be some kind of fictional creature that would fit the current plot line.

We found us a hound dog and named him Baskerville (of *The Hounds of Baskerville,* of course). He certainly lived up to his emulation.

Basker, as we called him, was part hound, part wild beast. We picked him out of the litter because he had a sort of regal sense about him, as if he really was pulled out the pages of a book in order to become a part of our story. He was a reddish-tan color and had large floppy ears (apparently, we had a thing for ears that flop) that were warm and as soft as velvet. My brother would ride him like a horse and rub his ears like a blankie. They were buds.

But sometimes, Basker would hear a different calling. It would stir in him as he sat at the top of our property, raising his head to the hillsides behind us, howling like a night creature or a sad lover lost; unable to find balance.

Basker would disappear for weeks on end, only to reemerge a coyote-scarred, fatter, smugger version of himself—content, and loaded with massive bulging ticks that had implanted their heads into him, slowly sucking the life out of him, if that were possible.

We would pour camphor oil on the ticks until they suffocated to the point of pulling out. That became a ritual we tended to after Basker's explorations over the Indian hills—and a couple of times on my brother as well!

(Once, my dad even got a tick. It was in the center of his chest and it got so infected that nearly his whole chest turned red. Dad would swear the rest of his life that he contacted Lyme's disease from that tick.)

Basker claimed the scorn-scarred hills as his own territory. He did the same with our musky carpet, with my brother snuggled into his side. He was a wonder, with a wet nose, a muscle-carved lion form, and warm, blankie ears.

One day, he went out on one of his Lewis and Clark adventures. It was a dark, Moorish kind of day, on the cusp of winter's end. Derrick wanted him to stay, but Basker was feeling the call again and nothing could stop him. Derrick pressed his face into Basker's ears and Basker licked Derrick's face. As Basker took to the hills for the last time, he looked back and howled for his small companion. Derrick howled back, and Basker was gone, never to reemerge. It's how he would have wanted it.

My brother would often sit at the top of our property, his eyes to the hills, like a lover lost, aching for his warm-eared companion. Maybe he still howls across the landscape, and my dad bellows back at him; a heavenly banter.

Chapter 16: Illegal in the Barn

Spring had arrived once again, and we began construction on the cellblock once again.

The porch was a totem pole Disneyland, with chipped varnish and hidden meanings, but adobe is another thing altogether. It was not easy to work with, so we decided to demolish it and start over. However, we had to live in the midst of this reconstruction, so all of life became meshed together with chunks of adobe and plywood. It was a cross-section of worlds. We all became hammer-slingin', rooftop-cussin' construction workers.

My brother even had a little tool belt just like Dad's. Sometimes, as previously mentioned, that would be all he would wear—well, that, and his cowboy hat and boots, of course.

We were to start with the kitchen, and then expand out, to create bedrooms where there were none. There's a sense of renewal to fresh wood planks. It creates hope and makes life smell like

Christmas tree lots. Although we were pretty over-the-top, awesome construction workers, it was inevitable that hired help would become a dire necessity.

Enter Barn Resident Number Three.

His name was Manuel. He just showed up one day. He appeared with a hammer, faded fringed jeans, and a jacket that could tell stories. He worked steadily, with focus, speaking not a word, until he would retire to the shanty part of the barn that we had deemed inhospitable for the goats.

He worked side by side with us, but in a dimension all his own. He seemed to defy the norms of what a human workday should encompass. Like a sweatshop factory machine, he would pound and cut and lift, and then, at the end of the day, along with the sun, he would disappear behind the shed pile to his barn quarters.

Every evening on the ranch, we would take turns making dinner. We all had our predictable stand-bys. Lauren would usually make some kind of omelet or tacos. I would make some funky casserole or tacos, and Dad would make his British borscht that tasted like cabbage broth and felt like some kind of "home for strays" comfort food, or tacos.

On one non-descript evening, it was my turn to make dinner. I decided to mix it up a bit and branch out, so I made a pot of chili.

I waited and waited for everyone to get back from Borrego (the small, low desert town we would trek down to for supplies, *Dos Equis*, and tacos), but no one showed up. I was in our deconstructed wilderness alone for the evening with no one around but Manuel.

Nights are like a black hole in the desert. They are Simon and Garfunkel silent; the kind that stand at the door of your breath, waiting. I was all alone with my chili and all the little howls and night movements of the nocturnal phantoms. Then I realized Manuel was there.

I wondered if he was feeling the *Sounds of Silence,* too. I began to wonder if he had a life outside of our barn; a life with a pretty petite *Señorita* who had red lips and deep eyes, whom he longed for right around this time every night.

I filled two bowls, grabbed spoons, and began the "hundred-mile" climb into the black darkness toward the barn straight ahead.

I knocked first, on a wood post.

Manuel sat straight up. He pushed some kind of book under his wool blanket. He was still dressed in his well-worn work clothes that were more like his skin by now.

"Hello. *Hola*. Um, I thought you might be hungry so…" I held out the bowl of chili.

"*Gracias, Gracias*." He looked up and I saw his eyes for the first time. They were National

Geographic eyes. He dropped them before I could read further.

"Do you mind?" I asked as I motioned to the blanket. He cleared the best section and motioned for me to sit.

"*Sí, sí,*" he said, and then there were nothing but the sounds of the nocturnal animals once again.

This was a different kind of silence now, the kind that spans all the gaps of the world; the kind that both separates us and joins us. It's those moments where two worlds try to rest cotton shirt sleeves together that we itch for commonality to smell like generic humans that simply need each other. There was a cryptic form of conversation in the clink of spoons in bowls and a nod of the head here and there.

After we had already shared our meal together, Manuel said, "*No hablo Inglés…*"

He had finished way before me, as this food was his daily bread and I'd already had mine twice.

I laughed a little and said, "That's okay." I patted my chest, "*Me no hablo Español.*"

He smiled, an immigrant smile, with less teeth than a man his age should have, but it warmed the silence and I was not alone.

I decided to attempt the linguistic gap.

"Um… *Que pasa?*" I had heard this phrase thrown around the work site. Dan would use it with everyone. Hispanics as well as his motley juvenile construction crew were included in this phrase, so I thought I'd try it out. He grinned and I was suddenly aware of our age gap. I was now a small child, not the white man's daughter. It seemed to equalize the playing field and personal guards were diffused for a moment.

"*Bueno,*" he nodded.

I picked up my bowl and he held his out to me. As we both held onto his bowl (he was hesitant to let it go), he looked at me with more desperation than he had allowed himself before.

"*Uno más?*" He pointed to the inside of the bowl and put his fingers up to his lips.

"*Uno más?*" He said again, his pride less visible now. Hunger and survival often usurp themselves above all of those pretenses.

I understood. He was asking for more. More chili, more human comfort, more hopes and dreams; just simply more. I nodded and took his bowl. For a split second, I felt the warmth of his chili-bowled hands. I would refill what I could, as my bowl was also half empty.

LISA NORTH

Chapter 17: Robby, Rosie, and the Third Wheel

Our first, desperate, failed loves are often embedded in our psyches. They rest there, like dragons in their lairs, only to surface when other failed attempts at life decide to slam us. The awkward "I'm nothing, 'cause he doesn't love me" country songs start playing like broken records, skipping past the good parts and only playing the "loser" choruses. We are supposed to grow from those moments into functional adults who have functional relationships, but, more often than not, they just simply scar and wound us, leaving us insecure and hating all the perfect *chicas* out there who never fail and get to have boys for breakfast.

One year, during springtime, Robby and I were hanging out.

Robby stood out, like a shiny nickel. He was blonde everything—hair, smile, face, and demeanor. He smelled like clean houses, saw the world through rose-colored glasses, and he was mine. Well, at least, I thought so.

We would talk and hang out, on our bus commute. He would tell me of his latest dirt bike triumphs and I would relate as best I could, because I, too, was a cycle rider (out of necessity, but still). More than anything, he would talk, and I would look. I would stare at his bangs, marveling at how they would feather perfectly, like a bird's wings, every time he tossed them with one quick head flip.

One day (I'm not quite sure when the shift occurred—maybe I was the slow-boiling frog that doesn't know it's cooking), our conversation began to shift from dirt bikes and dog stories to the glorious Rosie, pride of the Rez. He talked about her obsidian curls. Of course, he didn't have the sophistication to see them like I did. He just liked her hair.

"Hey, Lisa, do you think she likes me? I saw her looking at me on the playground and I was so nervous, I just looked away. Do you think she saw me and now thinks I don't like her? Or do you know if she knows that I like her?"

This was now our bus commute conversation. Somehow, I got caught up in the whole dysfunction of it all. Like a barnacle along for the ride on a whale hump, I became a liaison to Robby's passion. Still, I could siphon off some of it, even if it was not toward me with *Eponine* flair.

I could still be the one that got to see and feel it.

Robby would share his deepest, darkest feelings and his heart's desires with me. Rosie didn't get this part of him. I did. She got the show—the mating ritual. I got the real Robby, but then I would shift and become Rosie's confidante as well. In hindsight, it was not the best idea, but it elevated my status just a smidge with Robby; a sad, pathetic perk.

"I saw him turn away, yesterday. I don't think he likes me," Rosie said.

I wanted to slap her, just a quick one.

I wanted to reply, "Of course, he likes you, you idiot. You're perfect. You're the girl everyone likes! He wants to smother you with whip cream and eat you!" But I didn't.

"Yeah, he likes you."

That was the beginning of my tragedy. Not quite Shakespeare, but life seldom is—at least, for twelve- and thirteen-year-olds.

"Did he say he liked me?" she would press, knowing the answer and just wanting to hear it.

This little diatribe went on for weeks.

I was their translator of passion. I got into it, actually, until I laid on my pillow one night wondering why I had that stupid frizz ball in the back of my head, too many freckles, and, of course, no hips whatsoever.

The little what-did-she-say and what-did-he-say inquiries were getting a bit monotonous, so I decided to spice things up a bit. Consequently, when the next "So, how do you know he likes me?" came out of Rosie, I had developed a plan.

"Well, he gave me this note to give to you." I handed her a note that I had doctored up with a little hyperbole and panache. Actually, maybe a lot of hyperbole and panache; this thing had to get moving!

I was starting to feel like my nose was growing large and bulbous and I was courting *Roxanne*, I mean Rosie, as well. It was all a little game to her, anyway. Robby was just one rung on the pole she would climb to the top. (Yes, I am using "pole" in the derogatory manner. But I was the one with the dice here.) They didn't realize that I was constructing this whole moment for their memories. I began to get into the drama of just at least being a bystander to first love.

Some days, I would play out their story in my mind. They would go to a fancy ice cream soda fountain, like in the movies or New York (because everything cool was in New York), and Rosie would wear a perfect, yellow, daisy print, calico dress. Robby would wear a gentleman's attire: white shirt, tie, and loafers. His bird-winged bangs would be perfectly feathered and her curls would bounce in slow motion.

The movie of Robby and Rosie was much more entertaining than the actual awkward "He said" and "She said" conversations that played out in reality. Pretty soon, I became keenly aware of the fact that lovesick Robby was actually pretty lame compared to dirt-bike Robby.

Still, I began to realize how invaluable "third wheels" can potentially be; much more than they get credit for. They can provide the balance needed in what would otherwise be nothing but flirty eyes and distant heart pangs with bits of strained conversations thrown into the mix. Besides all of this, they get the best view, without the pressure. Third wheels watch and learn how to navigate the crazy love road—at least, until it's their turn to steer. I wondered if and when I would be a two-wheeler, and who would third-wheel for me? Maybe, by then, I would have a handle on this whole "love" thing. I had lots of practice watching, at least.

Unfortunately, Dad's many conquests were not super helpful in trying to construct the healthy relationship manual, and Mom's newest happily-ever-after was not going quite as happily as planned, either. It was clear I would need to navigate this road myself.

I can still see Robby and Rosie, in my mind's eye.

Although I used to get great satisfaction out of imagining Rosie to be toothless, 300 pounds, with twelve kids, and living on the Rez, and Robby as fat and balding, with no more feather-flipped bangs, I now prefer to leave them back in time; perfect and fresh, with her curls and his white smile under a desert sun… and me, watching from a distance.

Chapter 18: Where's my Red Cape?

Although change is inevitable and apparently the daily gum-chew of life with Dad, I was not prepared to lose my constant companion. Once Lauren began her new commute to the high school, I was left alone. She rode the motorcycle to her bus and left me with nothing but my two feet to get to mine. That part was okay, by me, though. I like the world better at two miles an hour.

I contemplated the lizards turning to statues while they watched me watch them, and followed the crevices carved in the dust-packed, dirt road, as I sang the reverse of "Don't step on a crack…" (I'd sing, "Step on the crack… or you'll break your mother's back.") Then I'd think about my mother and I'd wonder if she was thinking about me. I wondered if she knew that we didn't have toilets that worked most of the time, or about the evenings that Dad had too many *cervesas* before he drove us back up from the one-horse town where we often got tacos.

During those rides, I would grip the seat and close my eyes, imagining we were flying off the cliff at 80 miles an hour and I was floating over the cactus flowers to my death. I wondered if she could hear my heart break when Robby declared his love for Rosie instead of me and if she felt my loneliness that would feed on my heart at night like bed bugs.

I thought about life in the civilized world, where there were no tarantula wasps—or even tarantulas, for that matter! I wondered if my mom knew that I was thinking about her while I walked on the dust-cracked road or that I missed her warm, freckled hands. Then, resentment crept in and I wondered if she liked having her evenings to honeymoon with her new man, while I was alone in my world of thoughts, desperately yearning for my grown-up life to start.

The great thing about life at two miles an hour is that time dissolves into mind treks and wistful longings. It's almost like reading a great book, except it's yours, and you can twist and turn it in any direction you want to. The advantage to loneliness is that you get to invent another story; one where you are a red-carpet beauty trying to decide where to vacation with David Cassidy—the Bahamas (because the dolphins are there) or Paris (because the crêpes are there). Before you know it, time has diffused into your mind stories, your commuters have arrived, and you're off to your matter and mass life—the one with school bullies and Rosie and Robby making out.

When the school day ended, I approached my dirt road and journeyed back home. It should have been just a simple repeat of my morning walk, but it was on a completely different plane; the one where "fight or flight" kicks your ass. There were no ponderings and wonderings or watching cute little lizard statues. I was in a stand-off of man (or small little girl child) versus nature.

Since our property abutted the hillside of the Indian reservation, the "lines" of whose property was whose often got blurred. Due to the fact that the Native populace were forced to exist on the Rez, we felt the least we could do was to give them some extra perks—like land upon which they could graze their cattle, extra fishing water rights, etc.—to lighten the load they had been burdened with.

Needless to say, cattle often found themselves crossing over onto our property, for a nibble or two.

White Bull Dennis was not the only bull from the pen to carouse our property (pun intended). Another group of horned, bulging beasts often roamed free on our land. They hung in huddles, smoking cigars and spitting out bits and pieces of other children they had gorged themselves on, I was sure. It was my job to get past them, each day, with my life and limbs intact.

I walked as all prey know how to—tiptoeing as silently as possible—as they eyed me, scratching and pounding the earth with their hooves, breathing out steam, and nodding their horns in my direction. We maintained steady eye contact as I mustered up all of my gumption in order to just simply get past them.

Their eyes would say, "Don't even think about it."

Mine would say, "I won't, I'm not, and you're all so pretty. I love you. If you would like, I'm happy to crawl across the dirt."

Oftentimes, to diffuse my nerves, I would recall a story my grandma used to read to me when I was little. It was called *The Story of Ferdinand.* Ferdinand was a sweet, loving, little bull that would rather gather flowers in his horns than small children. I would replay this story as I'd watch the angry crowd of bulls stomp and breathe in my direction.

I was always very cautious and strategic. I tried not to ever wear anything remotely Spanish bullfight red (or even bright colors at all, for that matter). I tried to blend in, which was kind of my norm, anyway, by camouflaging myself to look like the trees, the dirt, and the lizard statues. As I would pass by them, I noted, with each step, that I was, in fact, still breathing and my life was still in place. Heart pounding, I would start to feel a heightened sense of awareness. My adrenaline matched theirs, and I realized we were both in that moment together; in a predator and prey dance. As someone who awakens from a heart attack and appreciates their life more, I would reach my home, grateful for the broken-down little bit of shelter and the grand gift of solid, locking doors. Then I would be back inside my head, wondering if my mom knew that I skirted death each day just to come home from school. I wondered if she saw my courage or felt my fear. Then I would wonder if she cared or if, maybe, she was smelling her new life like I was smelling mine—full of wonder, and battles waged and won.

At one point, I shared these "bull" stories with my dad later in life. He got that proud British grin of his, and simply said, "Atta girl!" High praise, indeed.

LISA NORTH

Chapter 19: Renovation 101

When the world around you is "under construction," every day is a surprise.

I woke up each morning to the smell of pine, the pounding of nails, and droplets of water on my face from the unfinished roof. We had draped the ceiling with plastic, which caught water from the nightly, torrential rains. It was everyone's morning duty to empty it. This became our wake-up routine.

"Hey, Lee, grab the other end, would ya?" Dad would holler from atop his chair at the other end of the plastic. "Ok, now, careful. Let's empty to the left, into the bucket. Be careful."

"Ok, got it!" I would holler back from my chair position. Then I would bite my lower lip, and slowly and carefully begin to tip my end of the plastic. Then it would happen: Dad would get a mischievous grin on his face, and—WAKE UP!—the cold water would come dumping down, some of it on me!

"Awake now?" he laughed. He got a good kick out of this event.

"Hilarious." I would mumble to myself, soaked from head to toe. It never occurred to me that I had the same dumping power. I could douse him if I wanted. It just never occurred to me.

Then, the workday would start. We were a construction company. My sis, my bro, "ZZ Top" Dan, my new friend, Manuel, and I would begin the day's projects; all with Captain Ahab at the helm, directing his motley crew.

Other than varnishing the porch, we were commissioned to install the insulation under the house. Because Derrick was too little, and Lauren and I were just little enough, we got the job. Yippee! Fiberglass permanently resided in my fingers and nose and I felt like I had poison-oaked arms. I itched everywhere and non-stop. We were sent under the living room floors into the crawl space (where the king-sized rats lived!), with staple guns and fuzzy sheets of glass.

After that job was over, I decided I would never touch another piece of insulation in my life. I'll hammer, paint, crawl, climb, and lift; anything but that. However, at the end of the day, we would sleep a laborer's sleep; deep and pure, itches and all.

The next job commissioned to us stooges was to gather pieces of plywood from the stack at the top of the hill, where it had been delivered, and bring them down the hill to the house, so they could be nailed into forms of walls that would become our bedrooms. Bedrooms! We were pretty excited by this new construction job.

Another distinctive quality of our desert life included the times that the wind kicked up, almost to hurricane levels, sometimes even when little girls were carrying plywood!

There was a television show on back in the 70's called *The Flying Nun.* It was a favorite of mine. Sally Fields was the nun that could fly. It wasn't the jet-stream, Superman kind of flying; it was more like a slow, quiet lift-off based on her enormous nun habit. I just knew that if I could get my hands on one of those nun hats, I could lift off, too, and float like an angel does; an angel that looks like Sally Fields. Little did I know, I was about to get my wish… sort of.

We began to head up the hill to grab our pieces of plywood.

We noticed that the winds had picked up, but we were deep into our conversation.

"Hey, Lauren, do you ever think about Mom and stuff like what she's doing right now?" I asked.

"Yeah, I guess, sometimes, but we're gonna see her this weekend." Lauren said, always able to see the logical side of things.

"I know, but I mean the sort of day-to-day stuff, you know, like what Mom has for dinner, and who she cleans her house with on Saturdays, like when we're not there, with *Stop! In the Name of Love* blasting… stuff like that?"

"I know. I guess, but I love it here. Don't you?" she asked, and I pondered for the first time, really, as to whether I actually "loved" it here or not. Love is a pretty strong word.

"I don't know if I LOVE it, but… I don't know."

We reached the hilltop as the wailing wind continued to climb on itself, up and up, forcing the scent of raw sage into our noses. I breathed in deep gulps of it, letting it flood me to my bones, while I felt the warm, wet air currents lift my sweat-crusted bangs. We each grabbed a piece of plywood. We had become pretty strong and agile over the weeks and were convinced we could each handle our own piece. Besides, it would go quicker that way, and lunch was on the horizon.

However, we were about to add new meaning to the dictum, "Time flies when you're… attached to a piece of plywood."

Just as we got a good handle on our pieces, the winds kicked up to gale-like forces. I tightened my grip and, in the next moment, I got my dreamed-about, nun-angel lift-off. The plywood acted as a sort of a magic carpet, and off we flew! We went several yards before crashing down. We had a few scratches and bruises, but I now know what angels and Sally Fields know: flight is worth the scars it leaves behind.

We both lay there for a while, atop our magic carpets, laughing and breathing and listening to the wind rustle the ground, with our own thoughts rustling inside us.

"Hey, Laur?"

"Yeah?"

"I do, too."

"Do, too, what?"

"Nothin'." For a brief, airborne moment, I truly LOVED it there.

"You're weird."

"I know."

"But in a good way, you know, like Dad," she added. I would ponder that one for a while.

"Thanks."

Chapter 20: Something Strange in the Night Sky

As the construction progressed, we finally had a structure formed like a bedroom, and real beds! Our floors were still cement, and walls were pine sheets with nails, but it was ours! Lauren's and mine. I took the window bed, so I could look out at the night and the jewel-pierced sky. I was always a window-looker-outer. I loved the world that passed by through a three-foot pane of glass. It was like a painting or a slideshow. It seemed to frame the world in nice little chunks that felt safe, like small, escape packages that fit "just right" into my mind excursions.

On one of those fresh nights that pulsed with stars, we headed off to bed, but I couldn't fall asleep. I was held captive by my window package.

"Hey, Laur, what did you really think of Cecilia?!" I broke the bed silence, which was a bit taboo, as Lauren was not super keen about my nighttime discourses, because my mind would usually launch into the deep and often metaphysical. Tonight, however, I was reflective, so Lauren, always a good sport, wearily replied.

"I don't know. She was okay, I guess, but kind of annoying, don't you think?"

She had responded as I thought she would.

"I think she was sort of perfect," I said, bold in my reflection based on the exhilaration of the night sky in my three-foot pane.

"Yeah, I know, like in an annoying way, though. Like, why did she always look like she walked out of a magazine? And why did she act like she was our new best bud, when we didn't even know her, really?"

"I want to be her," I said, emphatically.

"That's stupid," she mumbled. I was losing her.

"I know."

"Night, Lee." Lauren often called me by only the first syllable of my name, as did Dad—and, I guess, everybody else, for that matter.

I laid in contemplative silence for a few minutes.

"Night, Laur."

I paused.

"Hey, Laur?" Apparently, we were not attached to the second syllables of our names.

"Yeah?"

"Do you think there's a God and Jesus and stuff like Nana talks about? When I look at the stars and stuff, I kind of think there is."

"I know. Yeah, I guess. 'Kay, I'm going to sleep now."

"Yeah, 'kay. Me, too."

That night, I watched the stars, shooting and dangling like earrings, and thought about the cosmos—at least, as much as I could frame it from my window bed. It was at that moment that I saw something that I will never forget to remember. I didn't sleep a wink that night.

The next day, when we got to school, Mrs. Johnston had the newspaper out, as we were settling into our desks.

I was still completely distracted by what I had seen, but I kept it to myself. I hadn't shared it yet, with anyone, not even Lauren. It was my phenomena—all my own. Plus, I wasn't sure if I might have hallucinated what I saw and was still sorting that out in my mind.

"So, before we get started today, class, I just was wondering if, by chance, any of you might have seen something last night, in the sky."

Mrs. Johnston knew what I saw!

I looked around to see if any hands went up. I stayed still.

"It was at about midnight last night, so most of you were probably asleep. Anyone?"

I began tapping my foot and bouncing my knees. I had to speak or I would burst.

I decided to risk the crazy factor and raised my hand.

"Lisa, did you see something?" Mrs. Johnston smiled. She could see I was about to explode.

"I did! It was a UFO!" I blurted.

Everyone laughed, except Mrs. Johnston. She gave her stern face to the class and everyone quieted down. Then she read the account from the newspaper:

"Last night, there were several documented reports of a strange sighting in the sky above the hills of Rancho Comesita. The sighting was reported to be around midnight and resembled an orange, glowing, oval ball of light that hovered just above the hill line."

She stopped reading to stop all of the laughter.

"It was orange and it glowed just like the paper said!" I blurted out, beginning to fill in the blanks. "I saw it! It hovered and it was big, kind of, and then it shot out really fast to the right, then it shot to the left really fast, then it bolted out of sight!"

I was now the center of attention, which almost never happened. All eyes were on me. There were more questions, as well as "oohs" and "ahhs," directed at me, about the details of my sighting. They even came from Lauren, who, needless to say, was pretty pissed that I didn't wake her.

"You wake me up for everything else!" Lauren complained.

To this day, I don't really know what I saw, exactly. It remains a mystery. All I knew was that it was my mystery; a nocturnal display that danced in my window frame and exploded into my myriad of quantum curiosities. Nevertheless, I decided some critical certainties right then and there, that "Yes, I do believe in God," and "No, I don't want to be Cecilia." Right at that moment, I just wanted to be me—at least, for a little while.

At recess, I think I wanted to be Rosie, Queen of the Rez, again, which was pretty much the norm, but she didn't have a UFO in her window frame. I wondered if she even had a window story at all.

Chapter 21: Barn Birth

When I think of a barn birth, I envision soft, fresh, morning hay; a groaning mare wriggling out her nimble little foal then licking it clean; and a brand spanking new, fuzzy creature, full of all the sweetness of newness the world has to offer. I don't usually envision a baby in swaddling clothes. Surprise!

It was springtime in the great desert; a time of flash floods and cactus flowers that turned the black and white world to Technicolor, all in a breath of a moment. I decided to go to the barn to visit my very pregnant, hippie cousin. I passed by the broken, crusty roof and the piles of fifty-year-old lumber stacks that showed promise of something grander for that sad structure.

Once I reached the back end, where my cousin, Christina, and her ZZ Top husband called "home," I realized that it did, in fact, have a comfortable homey feel to it.

Christina had painted the walls a pale, china-cup blue and set up a tapestry-covered floor bed. She also set up a small kitchen, with a dorm room fridge and trailer oven. In the center of her table was a bundle of cactus flowers, which brightened everything else in the room and put the finishing touches of a home qualification on their meager living quarters.

Christina had a glow to her. She actually looked content. She had stopped looking in her crystal ball to see the next chapter of her story. She was fine, thank you very much.

All my judgment diffused as I watched her maternally nesting in her kitchen, wearing her long, paisley, spaghetti-strapped tent that just covered her belly. Somehow, it all worked.

"Hey, Cous'," she greeted me.

The kitchen smelled of Tahini and curry with a glaze of patchouli. I stepped through the hanging, cinnamon-colored beads that separated the kitchen from the decapitated remainders of the barn rubble.

"Hey," I said, to break the awkward silence.

My cousin and I were not exactly close, maybe because of the age gap that was more of a life gap. It's worth noting what loneliness will compel you to do. Christina didn't know that she still personified everything cool to me, or that she was my first real leap into true adulthood.

She had taken me to my first rock concert—*The Rolling Stones' 1978 "Tongue" (Licks) Tour*, where I saw Mick Jagger strutting his stuff across an Anaheim stage.

I can still smell the sweet, smoky air and see the dancing dreadlocks and beards, but my best Christina memory was a simple little drive to Laguna Beach, with the wind from her convertible blowing my hair and Carole King singing about it all being too late.

I didn't know what she meant, back then. Now, the song feels melancholy and nostalgic, like all good sink-into-your-soul-songs should. It was a simple day, but one of those kind that fill you with potentiality and immortality; the junk food of youth.

"Hey, want some scrambled eggs?" she asked.

"Yeah, sure, but let me make them. You should sit or something," I said, sounding all nurturing and such.

"Nah, I'm good. I'll make us some tea, too," she said. All of us being kin to that little island that ruled the world, a cup'a tea was like saying hello in British. "I have to move. I'll explode, if I just sit." She started preparing my tea with as much grace as a seal; smooth and fluid as fluid as a pop belly can be.

"Hey, Christina, so how are you and Dan getting to the hospital and stuff?"

"Oh, you didn't know? We're having it here. We have a great midwife and she's awesome. She just lives up the road."

Up the road, as in where my pig-butchering, goat friends live? I suddenly had a flash of pig intestines and a baby falling out of a mama goat's back end onto the barn floor. The sickening smell of metallic blood and gamey warm goat's milk came rushing to my sensibilities.

I wanted to say, "Of course, you are, but are you crazy?"

I suddenly felt nauseous. Not only was our barn being used as a home for hippies and illegals, but now it was a hospital! I couldn't believe she was going to bring a tiny newborn into this infection-crusted landfill. Even the dangling, cinnamon beads and cactus flowers couldn't change that.

What was she thinking?

Despite my incredulity, all I could manage was, "Thanks. This is good tea. What is it?"

"Patchouli."

Of course, it was.

On a spanky, crisp, spring morning, we awoke to the far-off, distant sounds of life. Little May Dawn was born at 4:00 AM.

She was wrapped in swaddling beach towels and was like a nimble little foal, with a furry head and resilient eyes that were the same color as the walls of her new home. She smelled of something warm and fresh, like cactus flowers and biscuits, and something a little patchouli-like; all of the newness and sweetness the world has to offer.

That barn must have had a blazing star hovering above it that night.

LISA NORTH

Chapter 22: The Boy Who Lived in a Shoe

The London stage holds a plethora of artful images: Shakespeare, famed musicals, Monty Python, and—not to be overlooked—my little, 4'9" British nana, who used to perform her many oratories and monologues there.

But none were as captive an audience, I'm sure, as us grandkids. My favorite monologues of hers were *A Lesson with a Fan*, about a flirtatious moment interspersed with a temptress fan, and the tragic love story of *Lee Fang Foo,* to which, at the dramatic end of one of her many performances on Sunday afternoons for us, she would *faux* slice her throat with her index finger, ever so slowly, so as to emphasize the dramatic effect, indicating the poor, love torn character's fated end.

We would listen attentively, drawn in by this little powerhouse of a woman in all her drama and feistiness. Then we would plead long and hard, afterwards, for her to remove her false teeth and give us her old British hillbilly impersonation. We would laugh until our stomachs hurt.

We never told her, so as not to bruise her prominent and delicate ego, that *Lee Fang Foo* was our favorite of her monologues, for sure, but nothing could top the false teeth out on the counter and her gums-a-bobbing mimicry of an old gypsy.

My nana was an itty, bitty little thing on stilts. Topping out at a whopping four-foot-nine, she never went anywhere without her five-inch platform heels on.

"One inch shorter, and she would have been a dwarf," my cousin would tell me with panic in her eyes, as she only beat that height by an inch or two herself. Of course, this would set my mind to wander into fairytales and odd characters of old. Some of those idiosyncrasies actually began to explain my family with new clarity. (We were an odd bunch, and something had to explain it.) The thought came to me that I might possibly be related to dwarves and then wondered if Narnia hid behind Nana's wardrobe of caftan dresses that we, as kids, would play dress up in.

Along with her petite frame and heels, Nana never went anywhere without her heavily sculpted white wig that I would later discover covered her almost balding head. My dad must have gotten his "hair", or lack thereof, from her, because my grandpa had a full head of hair, much to Dad's chagrin that he might inherit anything from his mother. But it was her creamy, illustrious, baby-buttress skin that she was most proud of, as she would point out at every visit. It was the result of 40 years of POND'S® Cold Cream, and handfuls of Shaklee's vitamins that she took religiously (literal pun intended) each day. We were DNA recipients of these elegant genes—peaches and cream skin, balding heads, and, of course, bad English teeth.

"Have us a feel, Love" she'd say, in her full British accent that she refused to give up to the Americas, as she would put my hand up to her cheek that seemed to resemble what I always thought a dolphin might feel like.

"I don't look a day over sixty, do I?" she'd beg, in her self-assured tone.

"Yeah, you look amazing, Nana," was always the correct response. "Good" or even "great" would not suffice; "amazing" was the only right answer to her subversively rhetorical question.

Then we'd put egg whites on our faces to dry, so that our pores would shrink. It was the facial of British royalty, apparently. I never really could see my pores, so I wasn't sure why I needed to shrink them, but I thought it was fun to tighten my face until I couldn't talk.

"Don't say a thing," she would murmur, "or else you'll crack your face."

I wasn't about to crack my face!

Then we'd wash it off and she'd repeat, "Have us a feel. Have you ever seen a baby with as smooth a cheek as mine?"

"No, not ever, Nana," I'd say, and then we'd be best buds, for at least five minutes, which is an eternity for British affections.

Nana was religious, to the tenth power. Practically every word out of her mouth was about God. This both fascinated me (I myself was in a contemplative state at this time as to God and His hidden, yet profusely present, attributes) as well as confused me. Boy, could she bust out the hymns. She would sit down at the piano and belt out *How Great Thou Art* like Ethel Merman. She was a kick—a bit staunch and comically vain, yes, but a kick.

Nana, however, would never have dared to venture out to the ranch. It was not dignified enough, I guess. Either that, or she was never invited. It was probably the latter; there were only polite affections between my father and his mother.

They tolerated each other, at best.

Even at her deathbed, she had the last word, according to my dad.

He had gone to visit her in the hospital. As the curtain was closing, she pulled him close when he asked her if she needed anything.

Her words were, "What I wouldn't give for a good shit," and then she chuckled as best she could, being at her last moments.

A good Brit holds their humor to the last, but she also held a vice-grip on my father's patience, even long after her death.

The furthest Nana would venture toward our neck of the woods was to my uncle's church, 20 miles away. My uncle was charismatic. He had a tilted smile and an intentional "lean-in," when he'd meet someone. He'd take your hand and look as if everything you had to say was brilliantly important, but for the distance in his eyes, you'd be convinced of that fact. He would deliver television-like Evangelist sermons that could shake the rafters as well as you in your shoes. He had the mannerisms, the hair, and the wide-rimmed glasses of a "Billy Graham," along with a severity that felt like a cold wind. I never much wanted to be in a room alone with him, not even a holy room.

Then there was my aunt, whom, to my fascination, could click gum like nobody's business. She would pound the piano keys like a cheerful *Phantom of the Opera,* and then "grin-sing" hymns alongside my uncle. She had charisma all her own, too. Like a swinging hypnotist's watch, she'd draw you in. That is, until she was done.

When she was done, she was done. She had dark, plastered hair and a large bosom. Her breasts looked the same with or without a bra, which was quite mesmerizing to one who was in the new formations of her own set.

Mostly, though, I remember her hats; leftover British embellishments, no doubt. With my nana and her caftan, monk dresses and my aunt in her sleek hats, I knew my family was uncommon, to say the least. I should have felt some kinship to that, but I never did. I was the alien in the room, always. A fascinated alien, mind you, but isolated in my own world nonetheless.

After "the show" (i.e. church service), we'd mingle at my aunt's house while they unraveled from their smiles and drank a little. My nana would sip sherry and sing. I found it intriguing that they all could be so different, from one place to another.

It was at my uncle's little white church on the hill, however, that I fell in love once again. There was a boy that belonged to a family of one mom and nine other siblings. He was the oldest, at 15, and was dating my sister, which simply added to the melodrama of my soul. But I loved him from afar—the best and worst kind of love for a twelve-year-old. While my ear-to-ear grinning, gum-clicking aunt would pound out hymns, I'd stare at that boy I just knew would be my husband one day, even though he sat arm in arm with my sister.

Church summers are full of potlucks filled with cheesy casseroles and 13-inch pans with Cool-

Whipped Jell-O desserts. They marked the weeks with a reminder of just how fleeting our existence is. The sermons would set some foreign ache in my heart for those grand billows of God, but were always debilitated by the promise of merit badges if we'd simply fill the offering plate and maybe vacuum the church after the Sunday services. At least, that's what I perceived, sitting in my uncle's pews. Somehow, those billows were renewed when I'd look at the boy-man with Elvis hair and a wide smile. He was the man of this large, fatherless house, and he took this on with a father's protective covering. His family took up a whole pew and his mother held onto my uncle's sermons as if she were clinging to a precipice. I would sometimes watch her, when I wasn't distracted by my future husband's hair. There was something in her eyes that always made me rethink the full plate and vacuum thing. I wouldn't learn what that was until much later, when I would sing *Amazing Grace* and actually feel it down in my bowels.

Summer was ending and there was a fall fierceness in the air, the kind that lets you know that the "winter of our discontent" (i.e. school) was on the horizon.

There was an extra chill in the air, however, one Sunday morning. When we arrived at church, everyone was congregating around the "mother that saw God," with weeping and mourning faces. I felt like there was cotton in my gut. I knew. I just knew. Something was not right in the beautiful boy-man's family. Later, we would hear the details.

He had been out, chopping down a tree. It fell on him and crushed him. It was simple, to the point—beautiful, really; tragic and dramatic, just how a hero should go. All deaths should be so elegantly simple, but life, for his mother, would never be simple, not even for a moment, ever again.

When the time for the funeral came, I wept unabashedly, which, looking back, may have been slightly inappropriate, as this was a secret affair between me, myself, and… that's about it. My sister stood, silent; sucked in and inside herself. His mother looked like the pure and desolate *Madonna without Child*, and the church parking lot, usually full of beige floral patterns and polyester, was a black oil spill; the kind you try to hide under your car.

I watched my aunt become her "home" self and my uncle lost his televangelist posture. I looked over at my nana, who seemed to be lost in her own sparse memories of possible loves lost or premature endings of some distant dreams. No tears, just distance.

I wondered if all love stories ended as the fated *Lee Fang Foo*; a tragic sliver of mortality. I wondered if she saw me see her.

I wondered if this "ranch" life, with all of its unpredictability, extracted too high a price. I wondered if I would ever love again as purely and robustly as I did the boy-man that left his life before it had even begun. I wondered.

LISA NORTH

Chapter 23: The Cousin

Bullies tend to be our mirrors. They show us our weaknesses as well as our strengths. I guess we should thank them, somehow, because we find that the inhospitality of the world lurks in all corners: behind bleachers; next to P.E. lockers; and, in my case, out in broad daylight, in the middle of a murky lake, in front of God and all His brood. It was at that time that I discovered that "humility" and "humiliation" come from the same root. Humility is the "what doesn't kill you, makes you stronger" kind. Humiliation is the "kill you" kind. I think, when you are a pre-teen, it's always the "kill you" kind. It's only on later reflection that those moments begin to develop a lovely callous of humility.

In my case, the bully just happened to be my kin; flesh of my flesh.

My cousin, Teri, had it out for me. I don't really know why, but it could have had to do with the simple fact that, in all of our family's dysfunction junction, there was still an abundance of abiding affection, and maybe it alienated her to watch. So, she would "pants me" in public places.

Teri was a petite little rock with thin, wispy, sun-blond hair and an insecurity about her that, somehow, she was never quite pretty enough. She was smart and could be funny, but she was my nemesis, nonetheless. Yet, when she wasn't taunting me, she was always presenting me with some kind of adventure.

My uncle and my dad had ventured into a "partnership" to buy a mobile home park in the middle of nowhere, which happened to be just down the road, about 25 miles or so from the ranch. It had lots of cacti and waterfalls were painted on the rocks above the pond that was called a lake. They subsequently attached a hose somewhere and relentless water streamed down the muraled rocks. In the dead desert heat, the water was so warm that it created an algae line down the spray-painted rocks. To say it was tacky would be an understatement, so I won't. If that wouldn't draw investors (whom they were desperately seeking), well, I'm not sure what would.

The property also had two man-made lakes.

The main lake was fairly substantial and housed bullfrogs large enough to eat you. I was convinced their nightly burps were the result of undigested humans that had ventured into the lakes at night—old humans, that is, because that was the obvious demographic of such a delightful setting. It desperately needed a golf course to set things right, but all the retired folks got was bullfrog-laden lake ponds and algae-covered graffiti. Nevertheless, this was our Shangri-La for the summers. We owned "Lake Hellhole Mobile Home Park," and nothing could stop us from dives off the deep end into the abyss of lake muck adventures. I'm not sure if my cousin had a death wish, but she was always challenging the little segments of "normal" we tried to carve out for ourselves.

One particular day was no different.

"Hey, let's go across the whole thing!" she shouted, with tantalizing fervor.

"Swim, you mean? Across the whole lake?" I said, panic spitting out ahead of my words.

"Yeah! Are you chicken? Bok, bok, bok!"

Okay, so I haven't figured out why that taunt gets to us so much. Chickens stand tall, to obvious foxes that try to haunt their coops, at least in Beatrix Potter stories. They run around long after they have been decapitated. What's more, they regularly and consistently birth objects way beyond the little feather-covered cervixes they have to work with. And their babies are called chicks—which, in the '70s, was officially cool.

"No!" I belched.

"Okay, then let's do it!" she said.

I wasn't sure which part of "no" was unclear.

My sister was the first one in. She was always game for whatever Teri was game for. Teri was next. It was like there was a pecking order, literally.

I stood on the edge, debating, chewing away at what was left of my fingernails, as I watched them make their way across the lake. Finally, I jumped in. I was doing just great until I got to the middle of the lake. Teri decided it would be exceptionally hilarious to pants me right in the middle of "Hellhole" lake. I didn't care that much at that point because I was barely hanging on by a thread, as it was. I was taking in large gulps of pond-scum water. It was filling up my ears and burning up my nose as well. The water's edge line was right at mine and I was positively sure a bullfrog would take me below it.

I once walked on the beach and came across a shore bird that was dying. I felt helpless. There was nothing that could be done for or to it; there was no time. I watched it do a back-and-forth rigid rocking as it blinked slower and slower. Then it extended its leg for the last time, and went limp. I was definitely blinking slowly and rocking back and forth, in a sense, in the middle of that lake; dog-paddling my way just to stay above the water.

Suddenly, Miss "I'm-your-hilarious-nemesis" cousin of mine swam up alongside of me, and said (at least, that's what I heard), "I'm here, little cousin, to make your life even more miserable and desperate, so that when and if you arrive at the other end, you will not feel elated but rather humiliated." I'm sure I heard a little sinister belch come out as well.

She then took my swimsuit bottoms with her and swam ahead of me, obviously to make sure she arrived first, so she could stand on the shore, bent over herself, busting a gut, pointing and laughing. Little did she know that I might just die right there, pants-less and ready to be burped up by the bullfrogs that very night. Had she known that I was about to join the bullfrogs on the bottom of the lake, would she have done what she did? Probably not, but ignorance is bliss, especially for bullies.

Much to my surprise, and possibly her chagrin, something happened. I rallied. I stopped flailing and gasping. I focused on the other end. I realized that I, in fact, was a "chick" that could make it. Little did I know that this profundity would serve me well all the days of my childhood and beyond.

I conserved my energy for a moment by floating and I thought to myself, *This is not how you are going to die; pants-less in a man-made lake full of algae and bullfrogs.*

Then I remembered a swim stroke my favorite uncle on my mom's side had taught me when we were camping years prior. He had told me to swim like a polliwog. I thought about the thousands of polliwogs we had caught in buckets over the summers. I watched them morph into alien creatures that were part fish, part frog, and part alien. They'd start out as something common and normal, then, as time would pass, their struggles to discover their frog-ness would emerge. Tails would pop out, then funky little frog legs. Although they looked like heck, they knew who they were; they stopped swimming like fish and started pushing their way through the water like the amphibians they were.

"It's called the breast stroke," my uncle had informed me. "You cup your hands and move the water down your sides, and sort of bring your knees up, like you're gonna squat, and push the water that way. Simple."

Okay, simple; I could do this. I started pushing the water like my uncle had taught me. I felt the water move past me and the energy surging inside me. When I arrived at the other end, Teri was there, dangling my swimsuit bottoms from her flip-you-off finger.

I emerged with such a grand smile on my face that she just threw them at me and said, "Whatever. So, let's walk to the gas station and get some candy?"

"Yep…" I said, and that was that.

Lauren had already made it to the top of the road.

We were lagging behind.

"Want to hold hands and skip?" Teri asked.

"Yep..." And we were on to new challenges, such as whether or not to get a fruit pie or Ding-Dong at the Summit Store.

I wish I could say that was an isolated incident, but there would be many more such humiliations from Cousin Teri. Fortunately for me, though, there were only just enough to grow my wings and, of course, expand my cervix!

LISA NORTH

Chapter 24: Planes, Trains, and Autopilot

After that life-and-death exploit, I often contemplated life while grinding popcorn kernels into the well-worn, granite bowl formations that were bored into the rocks of our infamous boulder-clustered fort, which laid just east of our back porch. While climbing in and around the cluster, we had discovered that archeological find (the Indian kitchen), along with arrowheads and quartz gems we thought might have been left by *Kryptonians* (I still had UFO on the brain, at that point). Life, to me, had become uncertain, unpredictable, and full of an ongoing fear that had become like a nagging companion you try to ignore but just become used to, almost like a mosquito in your ear. But the sweet desert silence was both transporting and isolating, and would illicit ongoing meditations on the philosophical. As for the transporting part, your mind could just catch an imagination train and ride it for a while, which I did often.

I had my life all mapped out: I was to have three beautiful, golden-haired children (with a perfect husband, of course), but not until I had graced the cover of *Vogue,* traveled the world as a high-fashion supermodel, and dated David Cassidy for a while, until I realized the life of fame and fortune was too shallow. That was the real-life stuff. Then, as quickly as UFOs divert to the left, I would wonder if there really was a *Willy Wonka* factory in England that you could visit or if I could meet my London cousins on my dad's side and find out what real Brits are like…

These are those "trains of thoughts" that are so crisp and delicious when you're a kid; where everything makes sense and could happen. Those are trains I wish I still could hop on with all of the matter-of-factness that comes with possibility. Probability never seems to enter the picture; just a robust "could be" or two.

One afternoon, I was in such a trance. It never occurred to me that my imaginations were about to become murky waters, as if bacteria were slowly seeping in, and childhood was slipping out.

In my mind, I was busy, grinding corn for my family while my hubby was out shooting buffalo for supper.

Suddenly, my primal moment was interrupted by the sound of a small engine airplane. It was far off, in the distance, but still within earshot. Reflexively, I looked up, to gauge how far away it was… and also to see if there was any skywriting trailing behind it; something like "You are my everything, Lisa. Love, Robby." That would have been nice.

Small planes were not super common around our parts, but not uncommon, either. Why I was so drawn to watch this one, I will never forget.

I stepped out of my fort to look up at it and I noticed a trail behind the plane, all right; not a white cloud streak but, rather, a frenzy of black smoke. I watched as the little plane wobbled and toppled, gasping for air like a butterfly that loses the powder from its wings while it struggles to live out its brief little life, flitting from flower to flower, only to end up like a drunk on the sidewalk.

The black cloud enveloped the small, two-seater aircraft as its wings wrenched back and forth. Suddenly, the nose faced downward and the plane plummeted to the ground.

I saw a burst of flame and that was it. The isolating quiet of the desert returned. I tried to free myself from a suffocating cocoon and make my feet run—to tell, to save, to stop it from happening. "Robby" went away, as did Willy Wonka's factory. I didn't want to be on the cover of a magazine because I no longer had three golden-haired children.

Mortality had just showed up—not the "almost" kind I had encountered in the middle of the lake, but the real kind; the kind that a mother of nine that is now eight feels; the kind I would feel here again, several decades later, the powder snuffed from my wings.

My feet finally worked and I ran to tell someone, anyone. It took what seemed like hours to reach someone. I don't even remember who it was because my ears were cocooned with my imagination and all I could hear was my heart thumping, blood flooding my earlobes, sort of like a bullfrog.

The picture of the mangled plane was on the cover of the local *Tribune*; the biggest news of the year. It read, "A couple from Los Angeles died today in a crash near the Anza desert, due to engine failure." I realized, that day, that engine failure has many forms and somewhere out there was a day on a calendar with my engine failure written on it. Like a drunk on the sidewalk who sobers up only when the pavement hits his face, "probability" instead of "possibility" began to take over my trains of thought.

I realized that this little slice of freedom we were all living was, in fact, a gift. The packaging needed some help but, nonetheless, it was a way to see the world—where life and tarantula wasps and sage grass and star-blasted nights and Dad were all wrapped up together—and that, somehow, some way, it was destined to fall out of the sky with my name on it.

I was growing up.

Chapter 25: All Good Things Come to an End, I Guess…

Although life had just begun to make sense in the elusive solitude of the wild, Dad was running out of money. It was as simple as that, so, just as swiftly as he had swept us up into this alternate reality, it was time to leave.

Dad had bought a practice, down in the valley of civilization, and a suit. It was official. We were moving.

We sold our green motorcycles and gave our beloved goats—Windsong, with her huge, goitered cheek, and her little offspring, Nutmeg—to our goat-raising neighbors. We had one last beer with our beloved Sergeant and his china doll wife, swearing left and right to return. Sergeant gave a shot glass of beer to Derrick (little did I know this had been their ritual on many occasions). Margie's lovely, cactus-flower smile faded for a moment and her eyes glassed up. She would be out there alone, now, with her beer-drinking Sergeant, and her garden, always a garden.

We had a barbecue of some hippie, alternative meat product called tempeh burgers, and goat cheese, my favorite, with Christina and Dan and their little springtime baby girl. For a moment, I had forgotten we were in a beat-up ramshackle place. Maybe it was due to the wistful Jackson Browne song playing in the background. Maybe it was due to a simple gratitude for this beautiful, crazy ride we had all shared together.

The night before we left, I joined Dad on his porch precipice. I just sat there, quietly, watching and seeing. This place was in our DNA now; both of ours.

"Are we gonna sell it?" I asked.

"No, this is our home. Besides, who'd want it?" he joked. Porch silence ensued. The desert vacuum had, once again, sucked the words out that you were about to say but didn't need to.

"Yeah, we still need to finish the waterfall bathtub." We both laughed. It had been the big visionary of the whole architectural endeavor.

"Right, and everything else."

I hesitated for a moment then said, "I've loved all of it, Dad."

He took my hand and we watched in quiet meditation for a while; astronomers, together.

The next day, we all packed up what we needed and left any "non-essentials" as deposits for return. Derrick drifted off on one last nomadic adventure with the dogs and the tarantula wasps.

Before we drove off, Dad stayed at the top of the hill for a long time. We all relived as much as we could. We breathed in the drunken sage wind, listened to the cicadas' eulogies, and waved to Margie in her garden window. I rolled the arrowhead over three times in my pocket with my sweaty hands in hopes that, like Dorothy, I would return home someday.

What I didn't realize then, was that I actually would, several times, for weekends. I even brought my soon-to-be husband there, years later, for a weekend. He broke his arm in a motorcycle spill and now has a trick elbow that helps him connect to the DNA we all share.

My last time back, though, would be Dad's final one.

LISA NORTH

Epilogue

My husband hired a bagpipe player to cry out Amazing Grace, my dad's favorite hymn.

After the service, and after everyone had recounted their memories, we all just sat there, as Lauren clutched my dad in a container, her knuckles white, marked with a number, in a twist-tied baggie with his name on it.

We all then began the long pilgrimage out to the ranch, past the fruit stands and trailer people on the edges of the world. Past the old, clapboard K-8 school where I had fallen in love with both learning—"Mrs. Johnston style"—and Robby. Past the Trading Post, where all the Indian boys and men would perch on the rail and cuss each other out, in between swigs, coughs, and laughter. Past the Harold-drawn hills, the dogs on the roads, and the solitary, lone General Store that doubled as a post office and had candy delivery service.

As we turned onto the dirt road, I stopped.

There was Caroline's house, with lace curtains and a white picket fence, standing out like a petticoat under overalls. I pictured her married and still loving her "glass half-full" life.

We reached the top of the hill and stood for a while, looking out at the ranch and all our memories etched in its tawdry hills and scrappy blazes of wonder. For the first time, I saw the street sign—Jackass Road.

Perfect. How did I miss it before?

It was always our stopping point to breathe in for a moment this strange and visceral place. So, it made sense to let Dad rest here, permanently.

We poured him out and planted cactus flowers. We said our good-byes.

As we drove away, I realized this was a place that chased and always caught you, just like the man himself.

About the Author

Lisa North is a graduate of the University of Washington. Lisa has written articles for a couple of online periodicals and was honored by the PNWA for her poem, *Grief Digested.* She is a high school English teacher and lives with her husband and children in the river valley of Snohomish, Washington.

Lisa is currently working on a book of poetry. This is her first memoir.

Made in the
USA
Middletown, DE